Kopp -
Pages 36,
Page 71 - M

48 - Lethbr- -ge

page 58 - Kopp - (Winnipeg)

The Siebert Story

Contents

The Memoirs of Helen van der Sloot

On the constant advice of friends, and especially Sr. Louise and Alfreda (Ursuline Sisters), urging me to write my life story, I came to the compelling conclusion that I must do it for the sake of my children and especially my 43 grandchildren.

Communism

I was born on the 14th of January in 1933, in a small Ukrainian village called Neu-Lebental, not too far from Dnepropetrovsk and Krivoy Rog. My oldest sister (in fact, my half sister; her father died when she was a baby), Rose Bauer, was born on August 15, 1929. Another half sister of mine, Maria, died as a little child. My younger sister, Lydia, was born on August 16, 1934, and my only brother, Reinhard, the youngest, was born on Jan 2, 1938.

Although we lived in the Ukraine, my family is of German descent, similar to most of the people who lived in the village. My parents, Rose and Jakob Siebert, along with my maternal grandmother, Emilie Zoller (whose husband, Adam, died of diphtheria long before I was born), were devout Catholics, and as such, they ensured that my siblings and I learned our faith as we grew up. In the Ukraine, however, this was not such an easy thing to do.

At this time, the oppressive Communist regime ruled the country. Whether we liked it or not, we all had to adhere to

Communist doctrine, at least on the surface- the government demanded it. This atheistic religion forbade any sort of worship, and so it was imperative that my family prayed in secrecy. We were not allowed to have any holy pictures in the house. No crucifixes or any other symbols of our faith were permitted. All of the priests were sent to Siberia, and all of the churches were confiscated by the government and were either converted to museums or destroyed. If a Communist agent suspected that a family was religious, or praying, or practicing any sort of faith, it was customary for that agent to come, usually late at night, and ask the father, the head of the family, to come with him. We all knew what that meant: they were sent to Siberia, where most of them died from exposure, starvation, or torture. My paternal grandfather, Jakob Siebert, and two of my uncles were, in this manner, sent to Siberia. They never returned.

My siblings and I were taught from small on never to talk to anyone outside of the family, including our friends, about religion, never to say anything against the Communist government, and to be very secretive about our faith. There were always people who would aspire to become popular with the Communists to advance themselves, or as we liked to say, "earn their little Red dress". These people often did this by tipping the authorities off about others who were religious or complained about the government, even if their accusations were not entirely true. Accordingly, we were always careful to watch what we said and did around others.

There is a particular story I would like to mention that illustrates how the slightest negligence in Communist Ukraine could have disastrous consequences. The details of this incident were explained to me later by my parents, as I was too young at the time to understand exactly what was transpiring. It happened when I was a little girl on one cold night in January, as a snowstorm was raging outside. My siblings and I were already asleep in our beds, when suddenly there was a knock at our door. Of course, my parents were very frightened, but they opened the door to find a man standing on the doorstep, shivering in the cold. He asked if he could stay overnight in our home, and my dad, of course, invited him inside. My mother, being a kind and generous lady, saw that he was hungry and tired, and she immediately went about preparing a meal and making a bed for him. While she did this, my dad spoke with the man, who told him that he was fleeing from the Communists. He stayed overnight, and in the morning he was gone. However, he left a beautiful poem for my parents on a small piece of paper, thanking them for their kindness and generosity. Somewhere in that poem, God was mentioned.

My older sister, Rose, had just started school, and by accident, this poem landed in one of her books. When she was in class a teacher noticed the piece of paper protruding from the pages of her book and he took it away from her. This man was a colleague of my dad, who was also a teacher. He read the poem and kept it. He didn't give it back.

After a few days, my dad got a summons to appear in court. He went first to Dnepropetrovsk, and after that to Kiev. There, they asked him many questions about the mysterious man who had appeared on our doorstep and stayed overnight at our place. Throughout the course of the interrogation he pleaded that he had done what anyone else would do, asking the officers what they themselves would have done in a case like that, when a freezing stranger asked to stay the night during a heavy snowstorm. After some time, he returned home briefly before being summoned again at least two times more, where he was again incessantly interrogated. Finally, he was sent to Moscow. After some more questions, the officials opened a door, and the very refugee who had stayed at our place on that cold January night came out. My dad was very emotional, and he felt terrible for the man, who quite possibly believed now that my family had informed the Communists of his whereabouts. He told us later that, at that moment, he would have liked nothing more than to disappear into a hole in the ground. He was mortified, but did his best to conceal his sentiments from the Communists, who might condemn him if they suspected any sympathy on his part towards the prisoner's plight.

During all this, another man, a government official, was a boarder in our home. Although the official appeared to be a staunch Communist on the outside, we soon realized he was in fact a caring, loving person on the inside. A lot of people had to do that to get a job. They needed to appear like a Communist even if they didn't necessarily agree with it all on the inside. He must have liked my parents very much, because he wrote a nice letter to his superiors on behalf of my dad, putting in a good word for him. Our family prayed the rosary, we prayed very hard, asking for God's intervention, and miraculously, because of the boarder's letter, our prayers, and, I'm sure, through God's Providence, my dad was not sent to Siberia and was allowed to come home. However, he could be a teacher no longer. He ended up getting a job as a bookkeeper for the village, and after that, things settled down for a while.

Life in the Ukraine

Years earlier, when the Communists came into power, they took everything from the people. They confiscated farm machinery, livestock, and property. The farmers were forced to give up all their land to the government, which used the land to create *cholchoses*, or collective farms that the people had to work on. Each family could have a pig or two, a cow, a calf and a garden. With that, of course, we had all the milk, the butter, the cheese and the meat we needed, as well as some vegetables that we grew ourselves and stored in cellars, although the government would also give each family a little bit of grain to grind into flour, which people used to bake their own bread.

We had a cow and a calf, as well as two pigs that we butchered every year. The pigs were usually butchered late in the fall because it was cold; at that time, we had no fridges and no freezers, so the cold would help to preserve the meat. Usually, when it was butchering time at our place, several uncles and maybe a neighbour would come very early, around five o'clock in the morning, to butcher the two pigs. One of my uncles was a proficient butcher, although not by trade, and he always came to help us. My mother was very hospitable, and she prepared a nice breakfast with home baking, which often included a Steusselkuchen and some other goodies, as well as a big pot of coffee for the friends and relatives. In the Ukraine, we lacked the luxury of having real coffee, and we used roasted wheat as a substitute to simulate the flavour. Most of my family had never had real coffee before, and so we didn't know the difference. However, my mother had enjoyed real coffee from before the Revolution, and sometimes told us how she would have liked to have some again for occasions like these. Despite the absence of genuine coffee, however, everybody was always in a good mood that morning, I remember that.

Our parents, of course, did not want us young children to see the actual slaughter, but we had a general understanding of what transpired. All the men went out, caught the pig, and killed it. After that, they hung it up, scraped off the bristles with a knife, cut open the belly, and took out the heart, intestines, stomach, and liver before taking off the skin and carving out the different cuts of meat.

The women were very busy in the house that day, grinding, cooking, and preparing the meat for preservation. First, the intestines were cleaned. They were turned inside out and scraped and scraped. Then they were washed with soap and water and rinsed in the sink. These would be used as skin for the sausages, and we made a lot of sausages. The liver was cooked and made into liver sausage. We also made *Medwurst*, another type of sausage. The stomach was cleaned similarly to the intestines, but filled instead with spices and bits of meat from the pigs head, as well as other small pieces of meat and fat, to make *Schwarte-Magen* (*'Schwarte'* meaning 'skin' in German, since some of skin, thoroughly cleaned and ground up, was a part of the filling; and '*Magen'* meaning 'stomach' which, after being scraped and cleaned, contained the filling), or headcheese. The headcheese was pressed and then smoked. We rendered all the fat so that we had lard, and kept the crispy pieces that were left over, which we called *Grueben*, or krispal. In a similar manner, the pig's skin was cut up into very fine pieces and cooked. Nothing was thrown away. We even cooked the knuckles and added the meat to the *Schwarte-Magen.* And of course, we had lots of large cuts of meat. Some of these large pieces, like the hams, were smoked, while other cuts, like the ribs, were salted. We kept these in places like the attic or in cellars in the dirt over the winter, where they stayed cool.

People did everything themselves. Everything was homemade. We all had a garden where we grew our own potatoes, carrots, peas, beans, onions, garlic and radishes. We milked our own cow. My mom let some of the milk age until it got sour a bit. Then she put it in a frying pan and slowly simmered it until it got stiff, with kernels. In this way she made cottage cheese, which we used to make Kasenudeln, or pirogues. When I was a little girl, I didn't really like that cottage cheese, but as I got older I developed a taste for it. My mom also mixed hops into some flour and water and let it age to make the yeasty starter for sourdough. We baked our own bread. There was not much people had to buy, except for a little sugar.

The first grade that I attended was in Neu-Lebental. I have to say that I had a very nice teacher, a lady named Valentina Demitrovna, and I really liked her. She played the piano, and in December, she asked me to sing a Ukrainian Christmas carol while she played, for a little concert at Christmas time. I'll never forget that. She was a very nice lady, and I'll never forget her.

Liberation

In the fall of 1941, while the War was being waged between the Germans and the Allied forces of America, England, and Russia, the Germans occupied our part of the Ukraine. The soldiers liquidated the collective farms that belonged to the government, and all of the people who had lost their land to the Communists got it back. All the horses and farm equipment were returned to the farmers.

When the soldiers arrived at our village and replaced the Communist authority, we felt very liberated. Finally, we had the freedom to pray. As small as I was in 1941, I knew that under the Communists, we couldn't talk. I knew we had to be quiet, and to finally be free of that constraint and the constant wariness and fear that it instilled in us was so incredibly relieving. I still remember the feeling of freedom, a feeling that we never experienced under the Communists, as if a heavy weight had been taken off our shoulders because we did not have to be afraid. The Germans even brought a priest along to say Mass in our school, since we had no church. My little sister Lydia and I were so happy that we picked flowers and threw the petals on the path that the priest would take to enter the school. At the time, I found one detail to be very important, and I will never forget it: on the soldiers' belt buckles was written the phrase "*Gott Mit Uns*", which literally translates to "God With Us". We were so happy to have the freedom to pray and practice our faith unafraid, thanks to the Germans. However, in the end it turned out that the Nazis were just as bad as the Communists.

There was relative peace for a couple of years. We didn't have a hotel in the village to accommodate the soldiers, and so they billeted with the families. We also had a German soldier staying with us. He was really nice with us kids. Most of the soldiers were not old men, and they liked the little kids. Sometimes they gave us a little of their food, a little treat. None of this would last for very long, however.

Fleeing the Ukraine

Slowly, the Germans began to lose the War, and in October 1943, they had to retreat from the Ukraine. As the soldiers were retreating, they told all the people in our village that we should leave too, lest we fall back into the hands of the Communists. Our village was mostly made up of Germans, although there were some Ukrainians and Russians, and nearly all of us left. Only one family stayed behind.

We left everything behind and travelled by horse and buggy, escorted by German soldiers. After travelling for some time, it started to snow. We had a wagon and two horses, and so we needed a place to stay at night. We ended up staying overnight in barns. The people before us who were fleeing had slept in these barns, too, and they left behind bedbugs that bit us at night, and lice that laid eggs in our hair. Our mom would comb through our hair, picking out and killing any of the lice that she found. Despite her efforts, however, it was still very itchy.

About six weeks after our departure, sometime near the end of November, our wagon broke down at a place called Deraschnja, still in the Ukraine. We couldn't go on with the rest of the villagers. It was by the grace of God that a German officer came up to my dad and asked if he would be an interpreter for them. He said that, if my dad accepted the job, he would make sure that we all got on a train if it became urgent that we flee further. So we stayed behind, and they found a place for us.

We celebrated Christmas there. The Russians always had Christmas trees, but Christmas for them was just a holiday. There were no religious associations with Christmas, no mentioning of Jesus' birth. We stayed further and celebrated New Year's there.

Sometime in January of 1944, the Germans had to flee again, and they put us in a big truck and took us to the train station. We boarded, along with lots of other refugees. They loaded us into cattle cars, where we were packed like sardines. We took very little with us, only what we could carry in bundles.

Poland

After a couple of weeks we arrived in Poland, in early spring of 1944. We got off the train at a town called Litzmannstadt, or Lodz in Polish, where we had to go through a process called *Entlausung*, or delousing. The women and girls were separated from the men and boys and led to separate rooms. We had to take off all our clothes in order to get rid of two types of lice: head lice and clothes lice. They had to disinfect our clothes, and they also had to disinfect us. It was a terrible experience. I had never seen my mother naked before. They washed our hair in solvents and shampoos to kill the lice. It was quite an experience, but it was worse than that. It was quite an ordeal, let's put it that way. At the same time, however, we were happy to get rid of all the lice, there was no doubt about that.

We got back on the train, and after some time arrived in Frei Hermersdorf, a city in the Sudetenland which is now in the Czech Republic. We stayed there for approximately four weeks, where we were provided for by the NSV. Then, we transferred to Schwerseng, Poland. We lived day by day, not knowing what the next day would bring.

On March 1944, we arrived in Puschkau, in Poland, which is not too far from Posen, or Poznan. The Germans gave my family, along with five other refugee families, a big house to live in. It was a beautiful place, next to a forest, with a big garden that was divided up into six sections so that one section was given to each family. Up until now, the Germans had taken very good care of us. They put us up in Deraschnja. They made sure we were able to board a train when it was time to flee. They also put us through *Entlausung*, and they had given us this house. But the sad story is that the house we lived in now was taken away from a Polish family, a doctor with a wife and eight children. This family now had to live in a little shack on the other side of the yard. For us, that was a big problem. The Germans gave them nothing, not even a little section of their own garden. My parents were very sad about that. My mother always gave the Polish family some of the produce from her part of the garden, and sometimes made simple conversation with them; since the Polish language is similar to Ukrainian, they could understand each other. Now there was a Nazi women's organization called the *Nationaler Sozialisten Verein*, or more simply the NSV. Several members of this organization came to check on the refugees every once in a while, and when they saw my mother talk to the Polish people and saw that she gave them some vegetables, they were very upset. They forbade my mother from interacting at all with the Polish family.

In Poland we had rationing cards. We could get only so much bread, only a little piece of meat, maybe as much as one hamburger, for each week for each person. We had to stand in line to get our groceries, and with the influx of refugees the lines were longer. The Polish people were always pushed to the back. That's when we realized that the Nazis were just as bad as the Communists. They were people without God, and self-centered.

Just shortly after we got to Poland, my dad was recruited into the German army. All men and all teenagers, even boys as young as sixteen and seventeen, had to go into the army. There was no choice. After my dad left I would often have to get the groceries to help my mother. I had to get up sometimes very early in the morning to stand in line when it was still dark. Since there were no stores in the village, we had to walk to Unterberg, about two or three kilometres away, where, if we were lucky, we could still get some meat. We got our meat from the butcher shop. Sometimes, if we weren't there early enough, we'd go back empty handed. When we were asked what kind of meat we wanted, we always asked for meat with some fat on it because we were undernourished. In those days there was never any food left over. Nothing was thrown away.

We also had to go to school in Unterberg. We had to walk that distance every morning, and to get to school, we had to go through the forest. Because the war was still going on, whenever an enemy plane was approaching, one of two alarms sounded. The first was a regular alarm, and the other was a siren, a very fierce, harsh sound that meant we needed to find some cover. The siren sounded sometimes when we came home from school, and we had to run home. I have to say that, at those times, I wasn't really scared. I think it has something to do with our being a religious family. We believed in God's Providence. My guardian angel was very important to me, and because of that, I didn't feel like I was alone. Others were there, and that's what gave me the courage. I wasn't really afraid, and I didn't cry. Also, I had two younger siblings. I had to be strong for them. I felt that from when I was pretty young, from when the time that my dad left. My older sister, Rose, was not very healthy- she had rheumatoid arthritis. I was my mother's right hand, and I had to help, since there was nobody else who could really help her.

Orphaned

One cold winter day in January- everything happened in January-a German officer came and told my mother that we had to flee. The Germans were losing the War. There was only one train leaving to Germany, and we had to pack quickly and get to the station. My mother gave us each something to carry. She was very thoughtful, and remembered to bring all the important documents. We took what we could carry and had to walk for about twenty minutes to get to the railway station. When we got there, there were a lot of families huddled in piles on the platform. It was bitter cold, and we were freezing. The train didn't come for a long time. That's when I did something very stubborn. I looked at my family, freezing in the cold, and at my older sister who had just come out of the hospital, and made a decision. I told my mother that I was going to run home and grab some blankets and return to the station on my dad's bike. My mother was very worried that the train would come before I got back. I was aware of that possibility, too, but in my mind, I knew that it would take a long time to herd everybody into the train. I believed that, with the bike, I would be able to come back in time. And so I went, and thanks be to God, I made it back in time. They were all still there when I returned with the blankets on the bike. After a while, the train came, and we boarded.

The train was filled with refugees. Although everyone was tired, we all had to stand. Only the old people and pregnant mothers could sit. As we travelled, we would often hear news that a train full of refugees was hit by a bomb, and that everyone on board was killed. We knew it could happen to us at any time, any minute. We travelled throughout the night.

The next day, the train stopped at several railway stations. At every station we stopped at, my mother wrote a postcard to my dad, addressing it to his serial number for the army, so that he would be able to know where we were, as he didn't know we were fleeing. Both my sister and brother were getting very thirsty, and everybody was tired.

At one particular station, the train stopped and my mom went out to get some water for us. However, she did not get back in time and the train left without her. That was a very difficult time for us. With my older sister being sick, and with two younger siblings, I knew that I was in charge. I thought that we would be orphans, but at least we would stay together. We travelled alone like this for another day and a half or so. Later on, one of the ladies on the train came up to us and told us that she saw our mother at the window of one of the trains that just passed us. Despite myself, I couldn't get excited, because it seemed too good to be true. I thought the woman was just trying to cheer us up, and I had already resigned myself to the reality that we would be orphans.

After several hours, our train stopped, and lo and behold, my mother came back to us. It was such a funny time; if I talk about it, I get emotional. My mother was with us. We weren't complete orphans after all. My mother- I always have to give her a lot of credit and respect- told us that when she saw that the train was leaving and that she couldn't get on it anymore, she remembered the number of the train, which was on the back. She memorized it. There were two teenagers who were also left behind, and she took them with her. Her train must have arrived at the next station before ours, and we ended up stopping at the same station at the same time, and we got back together. It was a miracle. We were so happy to see our mother again!

Germany

We arrived in Germany, and once again, the Germans took care of us and gave us a place to stay. Our new home was with a farmer in a town called Hajen, near the Weser River. The farmhouse was close to this river, about five minutes' walk. We'll never forget the first meal they served us: a vegetable soup with meat in it. It was so delicious, and we thought, since we were living on a farm, we wouldn't have to worry about starving anymore. However, the farmer was not so generous. We worked on the farm, helping gather stones and rocks from the field, but we often had to exchange our ration cards for sugar, and for cigarettes, since the farmer smoked. He might give us a little something every once in a while, but he was not very generous. He had two Ukrainian maids working for him, and my mother would talk with them. They milked the cows, and always sneaked us a little container of milk without the farmer's knowledge. We were very grateful for this; since my brother was very young, five years younger than me, this was a real blessing.

We didn't hear anything from my dad. We didn't know where he was, whether he was alive or dead, safe or in prison. We had no idea. My mother had written post cards at every place where the train stopped and mailed them. She also mailed a card from Hajen, but we didn't know whether he got it or not. We didn't know where he was, and we assumed that he didn't know where we were either. My mother was getting sick, and she got progressively worse and worse as time went on. She was worried so much about what would happen to our family. We were very worried about her, and didn't know how long she would survive. We were afraid, once again, that we might become orphans.

The War was coming closer. The soldiers were fighting in the forest that was across the river, very close to us, about a five minute walk. It was very noisy. The farmer and his wife went into a bunker. They didn't take us along. The farmer also didn't take his mother, who lived in the same house, either, so my mother went and got this elderly woman to stay with us so that none of us were alone. We didn't know what would happen, or if we would survive. The shooting was very scary. My little sister was on the floor screaming, that's how scared she was. It went on for a while, but finally it subsided. We looked out the window, and people were putting out white flags to show that they surrendered.

Reunited

It happened in fall. One day, I went with my friend, Nellie Bauer, to pick some wild raspberries in the forest across the river. We crossed the river by ferry, and went into the forest. We were there for quite a while, and eventually Nellie suggested that we head back home. I wanted to stay and pick some more, but Nellie had made up her mind. She went back in the ferry and I kept picking. After some time Nellie came back. She found me and said, “Helen, come home, your dad is back”. I thought she was just making up a story to get me to come along, and I said to her, “I don’t believe you, you must be kidding me”. But she was adamant. She kept it up, saying, “It’s true! Come home”. I thought she just wanted to go home. Eventually, I gave up and went back with her. I walked home, and when I came around the corner of the house, I could see that my dad was there in the window. It was a very emotional time for me and I had to cry out of happiness knowing that now my mother would be well again, since dad would look after her and after us. I will never forget that time and the way I felt.

After that, we didn't have to stay too long in Hajen anymore. My dad found a job with the English soldiers as a watchman in Hameln, or Hamelin, the city of the Pied Piper and so, in November or December, 1945, we moved to Holtensen, which was close to Hamelin and not too far from Hajen.

In Germany, school worked a little differently. After grade 4 in elementary school, a student had two choices: they could either leave that school to go to a middle school or a high school or they could continue studying at that same school until they finished grade eight, after which they could attend a vocational school. I would have really liked to go to high school, but I was a year behind. There was a girl's high school in Hamelin called Victoria Luisen Schule, and so, even though I was a year behind, I applied. After writing an entrance exam for them and passing all my subjects, I was accepted. However, I had missed one whole year of English because we had been fleeing, so I was accepted under the condition that I take private lessons in English during the summer holidays, which I agreed to.

I started the second grade of high school then. In addition to English, we also learned beginner's French. I liked French a lot. English was more of a struggle, but I passed. It was a very happy school year for me. I had lots of friends and we got along very well. However, I would only spend two years at that school.

By the end of that second year, a lot of the refugees in Germany started to emigrate to other countries like Canada, the United States, and many countries in South America. However, they needed to have a sponsor in order to be able to emigrate to this new country. My dad had cousins living in New Gem, Alberta, and in Springbridge by Pincher Creek. There were also several relatives living in Coaldale. One of my dad's relatives agreed to sponsor us. Before we could leave, however, we had to be inspected.

We went to a camp in Fallingbostel, where we stayed for three months. We needed to see a doctor for a medical check-up, after which it would be determined whether or not we were healthy enough to emigrate. Because of her arthritis, my oldest sister Rose had a little bit of trouble. When we were finally allowed to leave, Rose was not allowed to come with us. However, it was promised that, in three months, she would be able to join us in Canada.

In the three months that we were in the camp, we got to know some very dear friends from the Catholic church that we attended. They were very generous people, and they offered to let my sister stay with them until she was allowed to come to Canada. It was very hard for us to leave her so very far away in a distant country, but there was nothing we could do about it. We prayed that we would get back together in three months.

Emigration to Canada

In July of 1948, we took the train from Germany to Rotterdam, where we boarded a ship called *Tabinta.* I'll never forget how hard it was for me to leave Germany. I would rather have stayed there because I had integrated myself in school, I had good friends, and I was happy there. I would have loved to stay. But my father thought that we wouldn't have much of a future there, and that we'd have a better chance in Canada. So we boarded the ship.

We had supper, our first meal on the ship, and it was delicious. After going through the War, not having enough to eat, it was a real treat for us. My mother finally got to experience real coffee again. We were looking forward to having more of these tasty meals on the ship. However, overnight we all got seasick, and nobody wanted to eat. Our stomachs were upset, and the best place to be was outside on the deck, during the day. Aside from the seasickness, though, it was interesting, and there was a little bit of music and dancing for entertainment.

We arrived at Quebec City at the harbour. There, I tasted my first bottle of Coke, and it was delicious. From there, we boarded a train that would take us across Canada. We stopped briefly in Winnipeg, and then kept on going. After several days, we passed the province of Ontario and came further west, to the prairie. It was so bare, without any trees. I kept my fingers crossed that the train wouldn't stop here, and that we'd continue on to where there were trees. However, the train stopped in Bassano, and we got off. Our relatives, Tina and Henry Peters, were there, and they picked us up to take us to New Gem, which is now simply called Gem. They had a big family, too, and we stayed at their place for about a week. They were very welcoming and hospitable.

New Gem

In the spring of 1948, the Peters' took us to my dad's uncle, Aaron Koop, and his wife, Helen, in Springbridge. It was harvest time, so my dad worked very hard to help on the farm. After about a month, a farmer from Gem asked if my dad could help on his farm. He had ulcers, and needed help for harvest time. We moved to their place, which was a little house, a former garage converted into two rooms, a bedroom and a kitchen. We had two beds in the bedroom: a single bed for my grandmother, who previously lived with my aunt in Pincher Creek and came to live with us, and a double bed for my parents. My brother, Ron, had to sleep with my parents, while Lydia and I slept at the farmer's house. Lydia and I did some stooking, where we had to stand up bundles of straw for drying so that the grain could be threshed.

Every morning, we had to walk about two miles to go to this little one room country school in New Gem. There was one teacher, who taught students from grade 1 to grade 9. Although I should have been in grade 8, I asked the teacher to put me in grade 7, because of my English. I didn't have as hard a time as I thought, however, and soon I was transferred back to grade 8.

There were three of us grade 8 students. We became good friends and got along well with the little ones. One game I loved to play with all of them was called Anti-I-Over. For this game, there were two teams that stood on opposite sides of the school. One team threw the ball over the roof of the school, and somebody on the other side caught the ball, ran around to our side, and tagged someone. The person who was touched with the ball was out. The team who went out the first lost.

The teacher's name was Arthur Loewen, and he could speak German, which was a blessing for us, especially for my brother and sister, who couldn't speak any English at all. We had lots of jokes about how my brother pronounced English words, and my brother was pleased to amuse us. One word that he learned, "away", he pronounced "ayowaya". This is just one example.

We kept in touch with my sister, Rose, through letters, and after three months, she was allowed to join us in Canada.

She got a job right away in the household of a doctor named Dr. McLean, in Pincher Creek. They had twins, and needed a nanny and help with the housework. The job was difficult for her as she didn't speak any English, but she managed.

Coaldale

We stayed the winter in New Gem. In the spring of 1949, my dad's cousin, George Koop, who lived in Coaldale and had a beet farm, contacted my dad, telling him that he needed beet workers. He asked if my family could work for him, and we agreed and went to Coaldale. He had a beet house with no insulation. There was a bedroom, a kitchen, and a living room with a potbelly stove. It was bitter cold in the wintertime. We helped to milk the cows, and to thin the beets so that they were about a foot apart. It was a big job, and my back hurt all the time. I could barely straighten myself up. After that, we had to weed the field. The third time, we walked through the field and weeded out any weeds that remained. When the job was finished, we still had to milk the cows all the time.

In the fall, it was harvest time. In those days, everything was done by hand, whereas now, harvesting is done by machine. We had a big beet knife with a big hook on the end. The beets were in a big pile. We threw the hook on the beet, stuck into a beet, and hauled it from the pile. We put it in our hand and cut off the leaves. We had to be careful not to waste any beets, as farmers got paid by the weight of the beets.

In the fall it was cool and wet, and the job was especially hard on our wrists. The first day, after working, we thought that our wrists were broken, that's how much they hurt. Our mother tied cloth around our arms to make them sturdier.

In the fall, for the most part, we missed school. However, once every week, my dad said that we should go to school to catch up a bit, to see what we missed. It passed this way for three years.

Eventually, we moved to another farmer, named Harris, who was a little closer to Coaldale. We did the beets for him, too, and that year my dad bought some land in Coaldale, across from the Baker School, which used to be a high school. With a carpenter, we built a very modest house. We had my grandmother with us, and we had to give her a bedroom to herself. My parents had a bedroom, and us girls shared a bedroom. At first, we had no bathtub, and we used the area where the bathtub might go as a bed for my brother. Then we got the sink and the bathtub, and a toilet. We were very happy to have a roof over our head.

My dad was fortunate enough to get a job as a janitor. He couldn't be a teacher anymore because he didn't know the English language. He was happy to be a janitor, since he worked in the school. He loved the schoolchildren. He could speak to the principal, Schlemko, who was Ukrainian. Eventually, my dad learned English, too. We were all very happy, since my dad had a steady job, and we didn't have to work in the beets anymore.

A man who lived nearby, named Mr. Huber, had quite a few cows, so every morning before we went to school we had to milk them. We could see him with his lantern in the winter, walking to his barn across the street. When we saw this, we knew it was time to milk the cows.

I finished my school, grade 8 back then, in Coaldale. My teacher was Mr. Robinson, a very nice man. He understood when I gave answers even though my pronunciation wasn't exactly perfect. Then they built the new school, the Baker School, which was right across from our house.

One of my good school friends from Coaldale was a girl named Joy Nakayama. Joy took piano lessons. She was a very good student, and she played the piano very well. How I would have loved to play something! But my parents couldn't afford a piano, or to let me take lessons. Joy was Japanese, and had been sent to a Japanese-Canadian internment camp in Slocan, British Columbia, during the war. Years later, Joy- now known by her married name Joy Kogawa- wrote about her experiences during the war and was made a Member of the Order of Canada.

Father Verhagen and the Sisters of St. Martha

When I was in high school, in grade 10 or 11, the Sisters of St. Martha came from Lethbridge to teach Catechism to the Coaldale children, to prepare them for the Holy Sacraments- First Holy Communion, Confession and Confirmation. They had to stay with families, so we always had a couple of Sisters at our place. I liked what they were doing and I sometimes went along with them. I listened to them while they taught Catechism to the children. At that point, I had the desire to become a religious sister myself. That was my wish. If I wasn't going to be a teacher, then I was going to be a nun. I wasn't going to get married.

This desire to become a nun did not develop overnight. In fact, in Germany, I already had the intention to become a nun. I knew some nuns from Hamelin. I liked to go to church there, and I sang in the choir as well. When I met the Sisters from Lethbridge, my old intentions resurfaced. I thought that it would be really nice to be a nun.

The nuns only came once a year in the summer time, usually for about two weeks. There was another clergy member, however, who came to Coaldale far more frequently. His name was Father Verhagen, and he was a Dutch priest. At that time, there was a little country church in Coaldale, a mission church with no permanent priest. Father Verhagen came from Lethbridge to say Mass in our little church every Sunday. At that time, there were a lot of immigrants coming to Canada, and Father Verhagen, in addition to being a priest, was also the head of not only the Dutch immigrants but all the immigrants in Lethbridge. Although he was Dutch, he spoke German and English quite well, and he became a good friend of our family.

Bert

Every Sunday, before he had to go back to Lethbridge, my mother would invite Father Verhagen to have dinner with us. Father Verhagen could speak German very well, as he had learned it while he was in school, and my mother was very happy that she could talk with him. One Sunday, when I was in grade 12, he brought along with him a young Dutchman, Bert van der Sloot. That evening, we were all sitting around the table eating and talking. Bert told us about his family. He had five sisters and three brothers. He told us that his brother Wim was a priest in Holland, and another of his brothers, Kees, was studying to become a religious Brother and hoped to serve as a missionary in Tanzania. I discovered that he came from a very devout Catholic family, and that he himself was very well educated in the teachings of the Holy Catholic Church. That impressed me and gave me a good feeling; my Catholic faith meant a lot to me.

Bert also told us that he had studied for two years at the University of Tropical Agriculture in Wageningen, but had left due to a lack of finances. During his second year, his oldest sister, Mary, got married in Holland. After the wedding, Mary and her husband decided to immigrate to the United States, as they had relatives there who would sponsor them. Bert's father helped with all the expenses, and subsequently couldn't afford to help Bert pay for his education. Unable to continue his studies, Bert decided to come to Canada. He knew Father Verhagen, who was a priest from Boxtel, his home town, and it was through him that he came to Canada. In Canada, Bert first found work as a construction labourer in High River. Then he got a job in Lethbridge at the agricultural experimental station, which he really liked.

There was a reason that Father Verhagen brought Bert along with him that day, which I found out later. Father Verhagen knew that my sister Lydia had a boyfriend who wasn't Catholic (her future husband, Pete, was a Mennonite at that time). His idea was to bring Bert to Coaldale and introduce him to the family in the hopes that Lydia might take an interest in him instead (as it turned out, Pete, Lydia's boyfriend at the time, became a Catholic years later before marrying Lydia).

After we had finished dinner and they were gone, it was my mother who came up to me and said, "Helen, this would be a good husband for you", referring, of course, to Bert. I had not thought about that at all; it was totally out of the blue. I didn't say anything. I was overwhelmed. In retrospect, it was very wise. In the past, I had mostly talked about how I would like to become a nun, but this is what my mother said to me. Yes, Bert was nice and intelligent and came from a very devout Catholic family, and that meant a lot to me. Bert impressed me, but what my mother was suggesting had never even occurred to me.

Father Verhagen brought Bert along with him again, and we started to talk together. Eventually, we started going for long walks together. We started to kind of like each other. We would talk a little bit about the future, and that's how the romance started.

With the immigration, I had to help Father Verhagen. We went to Taber to accompany some immigrants from Taber to Lethbridge. There were contracts that needed to be read in German, and that's what I had to do. Bert came along, too. We were sitting in the car. I liked school very much, and I was good at most math, but I struggled with series and integral algebra. Bert wrote on a piece of paper, trying to explain it to me, and I looked and listened, but I didn't get any better. He kept this little paper.

In time, Bert left his job at the experimental station and got a bookkeeping job in Taber with Kors Lieverse, which was a big implement business similar to John Deere. The auditors wanted him to make a review of all the statements, which was a big job. While he worked there, Bert rented a room in Taber, but came every weekend to visit. He used to write me these beautiful letters every week- I've still got them all. And they were really nice, very poetic letters. I wrote back to him, but I'm not a good writer. His letters were much nicer than mine, and I'll never forget them.

Graduation

Sometime in the spring, near the end of my last year of high school, I was absent- I missed a day of school for some reason. That day happened to be the day that my grad class chose the valedictorian. The next day at school, my classmates told me, "Helen, you're going to be the valedictorian for graduation". They said they voted for me because I was not there. Needless to say, I felt very honoured; it was a very big honour from my schoolmates. I'll always be grateful for that. However, I was overall a shy girl, and I was very nervous about making the graduation speech in front of everyone. I asked Bert to help me make the speech. He did, of course, and I was very happy about that. I told Father Verhagen about my nomination, and that I was pretty nervous about the speech. He told me that I'd have to say it to an audience sometime, to get over my nervousness, and so in Coaldale one day I said it in front of him, Bert and my family.

We had a very nice graduation dinner. Bert, of course, was my escort. After some more speeches, we had a dance. I'll never forget that. It was a little hard to say goodbye to all the friends. I think is hard for every graduate because we all have to go different directions from then on.

The Unemployment Office

Just as I was finishing high school, in 1953, Father Verhagen told me that they needed somebody to help at the unemployment office. James Lynn was the manager of the employment office, including the service section in Lethbridge. He knew Father Verhagen and let him know that he needed some new employees to work in the unemployment insurance section. Before this, my intention was to go to university to become a teacher. But when I heard that news from Father Verhagen, I was actually very excited. I didn't think about myself; I thought that I could help my parents, because of everything they went through. It meant so much for me to help my parents. It might be hard for you to understand. I'll never forget that feeling I had after fleeing the war, leaving everything behind. My parents had nothing but a little house we had built in Coaldale. We had been beet-workers for five years. It was very hard for my parents; we didn't have much money. So when I was offered the job at the unemployment office, I accepted immediately.

Before I could start work, however, I had to go for an interview to see if I was qualified. In the interview, they asked me if I was Canadian. I wasn't. They also asked me- I have to include this because it's funny- how many people were unemployed in Lethbridge or Taber. I had no idea, but I said a number. They all giggled; it was totally wrong. At the end, they said they would hire me on the condition that I became a Canadian citizen, which I did right away. I went to the immigration office. They sent me to the courthouse, and they asked me some questions, like, "who is the Prime Minister of Canada?" I got my citizenship shortly after that, and was subsequently hired as promised.

As you can imagine, I felt overwhelmed to get a good job so soon after graduation. I was especially happy that, with the money I earned, I could help my parents.

When I started work, I met a young lady that worked in the Insurance section named Carmen Nielsson. She was very nice, and told me all the forms I had to fill out. There were many forms, and each had a number. When I started, I wondered, "How am I ever going to learn all these numbers?" It was overwhelming, but I stuck it out and, in about a month's time, I knew pretty well all the forms.

In the winter, when people were laid off, we had to go to different seasonal work places. We had to take claims from the workers, who stood in long lines, trying to get unemployment insurance when they were laid off. My main job was in the office at the counter figuring out how much money each unemployed person got. In the winter, we had long lines of unemployed people waiting to be served. It was a very busy time.

I was working at the counter where the unemployed people came to get paid. They gave us a slip which told us how many days they were unemployed and how much they earned. We had to use the numbers to determine how much money each unemployed person got. We wrote how much money they had coming, brought it to the cashier in the cage, and they would get paid. That was my main job at the counter. In the winter, when people were laid off, we had long lines of unemployed people waiting to be served. We were so tired standing for hours at the place. It was a very busy time. Sometimes, after the summer, we had to go to different seasonal work places outside of Lethbridge and take claims from the workers, who stood in long lines trying to get their insurance. The unemployed people in these towns got their money sent to them by post, but in order to fill out the forms, our people had to go to the individual towns. I was usually one of those who worked at the counter to help unemployed people from Lethbridge, though, and there were a lot of them.

The first salary, which I thought was fantastic, was $140 a month. It was a good salary without any education required for the job. I worked for one year, and then I had a chance for a promotion. However, in order to get the promotion, I had to write a test. I passed it, and they raised my salary to $200 a month. That was even better. I have to say that I gave all my money to my parents. I only kept a little money to go for coffee in the morning and in the afternoon- we all did that. I also gave some gas money to Pete, Lydia's boyfriend, who drove Lydia and I every morning. Lydia also had a job in Lethbridge; she was a secretary at Baalem Wholesale.

Pete had to go to work much earlier than we did. It was a good chance to go along with him, though. There was a church- St. Patrick's church- which was not out of the way for Pete, so Pete would drop us off there every morning before he went to work. And so we had the chance to go to Mass every morning. We attended Mass there, and then we walked to our workplaces. I want to say how fortunate I felt to be able to go to Mass during the five work days. It was such a blessing.

I enjoyed work at the unemployment office. Oftentimes, there were a lot of immigrants from Germany and Ukraine. Lots of immigrants discovered that I could speak German, and they were very nice to me. Some brought me presents. I don't know why. I think they were just happy to be able to talk to somebody in German.

Sometimes there were disputes between the farmers and the immigrants who worked for them, to the point where they had to go to court. One day, the manager, Mr. Lynne, asked me if I could go to interpret. I didn't mind at all. I knew German and enough English to translate. It was interesting; I always learned more. But one time, there was a Ukrainian beet worker who wanted to take his dispute to court. Lynne asked me to come again, but my Ukrainian wasn't that good; I had not spoken it for a while. I said, "I'm sorry, I don't understand or speak enough of it." I really didn't want to go, because I felt I couldn't do it. Nevertheless, Lynne insisted that I go, and he took me to the courthouse. I didn't really have a choice. At the courthouse, the beet worker started to talk in Ukrainian. I couldn't understand him. I would have loved to, but I couldn't do it; I had forgotten most of my Ukrainian. It was the biggest embarrassment of my life.

Married

Bert at that time was working with Kors Lieverse in Taber. One day, an implement salesman from Taber met Bert at the Kors Lieverse office and said, "You know, Clarence Weatherhead in Berdette has a John Deere dealership, and they desperately need an accountant. Would you consider?" The job Bert had in Taber was only a part time job, so there was really no choice. He said, "Yes, I'll take the job." And so he worked for Clarence Weatherhead at the John Deere dealership in Berdette. He really liked his new job. In addition to doing the books, he also had to work as a salesman at the John Deere hardware story. So he was a salesman and a bookkeeper.

After my second year at the unemployment office, in 1955, Bert and I got engaged. It was a very exciting and emotional time. We looked for a place to live, and decided to buy a little house in Berdette from an elderly Irish lady. It was a very tiny little house- really more of a shack- but it had a big garden. It was fairly reasonable; a living room suite with a bedroom suite. For the last three years, I'd given most of my money to my dad. After I got engaged, my dad said, "Helen, you have to save some money for yourself," and so, from that point on, I kept the money I earned. Together, Bert and I saved up enough money to make a down payment on the house. We fixed up the little house ourselves. We painted it, and put the wallpaper in it, which made it very nice. There was no running water, and no furnace. We just had to have electric heaters. But we made the inside just as comfortable as could be. We had everything we needed to live.

One year after our engagement, on the 18th of August, 1956, Bert and I got married. We were married in Coaldale by Father Verhagen and Father MacLellen. There was also a German priest present. It was a beautiful wedding. All my family, my Aunt Helen and Uncle Fred Kopp (from Winnipeg), Mary (Bert's sister) and her husband, Jook Venbrux with their two little sons, Henry and Jack and all our dear friends in Coaldale, including my friends from the Employment office and Bert's colleagues, helped us to celebrate. The Catholic Women's League always prepared a big banquet for the bride and groom, and it was held in the Parish Hall. My parents gave us a kitchen table and chairs for our new house as a wedding gift. For our honeymoon, we went to Waterton Lakes for one week. I remember it being very hot and I was very sunburned, especially on my legs because I wore shorts. Waterton Lakes still has a special place in my heart, from the Lake itself to the mountains and Red Rock Canyon.

In the beginning, I left the unemployment office and helped Bert with the customers at the store. I helped until I was about six months pregnant. Then I thought I had to get ready for the baby, and I stopped working at that time. We were very happy in our little house. It was very far from Coaldale, but we went to visit quite often, and my parents came to visit, too. There was no running water. We had a cistern outside, which we had to haul all the water from. We had to haul all the water in to heat it up in a big boiler, since we didn't have a furnace. There was a big back porch that was not heated, and that's where we kept the fridge. We didn't have a toilet inside, but we had an outdoor toilet. In years to come, we had a special pail of water which we used to rinse out the children's diapers, which we would then carry outside and dump into the toilet. We had no bathroom, no bathtub, but we had two of those big tubs for rinsing clothes, which we had to take our baths in, and a ringer washer with a ringer that could swivel. Washing clothes with the ringer washer was a tough job, and it was hard on the back. There was no polyester; the clothes were all cotton, and all the shirts, pants and dresses had to be ironed. When you think of it in today's terms, it was all pretty inconvenient. But it was comfortable, and we were happy.

Motherhood and Medicine Hat

On the 3rd of August, 1957, Rose Marie was born. We didn't have much money, so we had to use reusable diapers made of cloth. I bought a scrub board so that I could wash the diapers by hand every day in the tubs. One day, when Rose Marie was about three months old, while I was washing diapers I scrubbed my knuckles open on one hand. We had company that night, and my scrape hurt more and more. I noticed that I had a red streak going up my arm, which means infection, but I didn't dare say anything with company over. When they were all gone, I told Bert about my arm and he phoned the doctor, who told us to come right away. We bundled up Rose Marie and went to the doctor in Bow Island (about 10 km from Burdett). I was diagnosed with blood poisoning, and given a bottle of pills and some ointments. I took the pills, but in the morning I had terrible stomach cramps. Bert phoned the doctor again, and he said that I should take the pills with milk. I did, and it worked. The cramps went away, so if you are ever on medication and have stomach aches, I tell everyone to take the medicine with milk.

We lived in that house for three years. Then we moved into a bigger house with running water. There was no bathroom, just an outhouse. But the running water was such a joy. In 1960, by that time we had three children. Rose Marie was born in 1957, Bill in 1958, and Henry in May of 1960. In the fall of that year, in October, we moved to Medicine Hat because Bert wanted to take a correspondence course through Queens University, New Brunswick, to become a chartered accountant. He applied for jobs in Medicine Hat, and they offered him $200 a month. In Lethbridge, there was no opening, and although there was an opening in Calgary, it only paid $150 dollars, which was not enough with the children. We had no choice, and we moved to Medicine Hat, to a house on MacKenzie Crescent. It wasn't my first choice, but now that I think back, it was the best choice. It was God's Providence, and it offered more than we could offer our children in Calgary, since Calgary is a much bigger city and we would not have had to spend as much time driving children to music lessons- singing, violin, piano, theory and poetry.

Bert had to study for five more years, and in those five years we had three more children, one after the other. Jim was born in Medicine Hat in 1961, Tony in 1963, and Paul in 1965. In 1966, Marianne was born.

And then, in 1967, I had a miscarriage. I didn't even know I was pregnant at that time. We had just come home from the summer holidays, and the rhubarb was ready to be picked. I pulled one of the rhubarb leaves off and then started to hemorrhage. Bert took us to the hospital right away, and the doctor gave us the sad news that it was a miscarriage. It was very sad; I lost the baby, and didn't even know I was pregnant.

In 1968, I was pregnant again. The doctor told me after 4 months that I was carrying twins. In July, I had to go to the hospital. The twins, Gerard and Joseph, were born, but they were still very premature. Their lungs were not developed well enough, and so they both died. One lived for two and a half hours, and the other lived for two and a half days. It was very,

very sad. Father McLellen was the parish priest in Medicine Hat at that time, and he baptised both of the babies. I wasn't able to go along at the time they were interred at the graveyard because I was still in the hospital. It was a very difficult time for the family, and I felt very heavy-hearted when I left the hospital with empty arms.

In 1970, Caroline was born, and in 1971 Mary-Jane was born. In 1974, in the winter, we left MacKenzie Crescent and moved to a bigger house on 8th Street. It was very close to McCoy High School and St. Francis School, where our children attended. We were a happy family. We were not rich, we were poor, but we were happy. We loved our children.

Bert and I both loved music very much. I never had a chance to learn an instrument because of the War, and because my parents were not able to afford it. When our children were old enough to start lessons, we gave them all a chance to learn an instrument. Rose Marie, Tony, and Marianne learned the piano; Bill, Jim, Paul, Mary Jane, and Michael learned the violin; Caroline learned to play both the violin and the piano; and Henry learned the cello.

Bert and I and the children spent many happy years in the house on 8th Street. Over the years, each of our ten children grew up to have families of their own. Today, I am blessed with 43 grandchildren, and 10 great grandchildren and counting!

As it was since my earliest days in the Ukraine, family remains a central part of my life. As such, my life's story would not be complete without at least a brief description of my ten children and their families, which they have graciously provided here for the benefit of our posterity:

ROSE MARIE

Born August 3, 1957 in Coaldale, I lived in Burdett until I was 4, when we moved to Medicine Hat. I attended numerous schools in Medicine Hat, and in 1975 I graduated from St. Angela's Academy, Prelate, SK. Subsequently, I obtained a B.A. (French, Political Science) and an M.A. (Political Science) from the University of Saskatchewan. In 1982, I married John

Kastelic, a veterinarian from Sangudo, AB whom I had met in Saskatoon. We lived in Leduc and Sangudo during John's years of practice and then spent 6 years in Saskatoon and Madison, WI, where John completed his graduated studies. Thereafter, we lived in Coalhurst, AB for 22 years before moving to Calgary in 2013. We have 6 children: Angela (Alan) Goudman, Rachel (Mathew) Grubb, John, Tony, Gabriel (Grace), and David. In addition, we are blessed with 4+ grandchildren: Elizabeth Goudman; Anthony, Patrick, and Anne Grubb; we await the birth of Gabriel and Grace's first child.

BILL

Born October 31, 1958 in Coaldale, Alberta, William (Bill) grew up in Medicine Hat. He studied Violin Performance at UCalgary and at Eastman School of Music in Rochester, NY. In 1990, Bill married Aleksandra Danicic and they were blessed with five children: Michael 1991, Maria 1992, Paul 1994, Julya 1997, and Thomas 2004. Bill held positions at Medicine Hat College, Mount Royal University, and Carnegie Mellon University. As a violinist and pedagogue, he has travelled extensively in North America, Europe, and Asia throughout his career.

HENRY

I was born in Coaldale, Alberta on May 6, 1960. Later that summer the family moved to Medicine Hat where I was active in hockey, baseball, and a lot of music until I graduated from high school in 1978. My first studies and career were as a cellist. I studied at the California Institute of the Arts and the Juilliard School of Music. I had the opportunity to perform throughout Canada, the US, much of Europe, and the Soviet Union and East Germany before the fall of the wall. My second career was as a businessman. I studied at the University of Calgary and Harvard Business School. I hold designations as a Chartered Accountant, a Chartered Financial Analyst, and the ICD.D designation as a corporate director. I have focused on several industries: Real Estate, Hospitality, Energy, and Private Equity. I married my business colleague and best friend Sharon van der Sloot on June 15, 1987. We have a mixed family with three children: Quillan Quarrington (1980), Caitlin Quarrington

(1982) and Paul (1991). We have five wonderful grandchildren: Quinn(2012), Finn(2012), Archer (2014), Anson (2014) and Nova (2014).

JAMES

Born: Medicine Hat, Alberta (first one of family born here), 9/9/1961.

Jim was mom's "Little Fritzl". He grew up number 4 child. Being in the middle of 5 boys in a row in the family, there was always a game of road hockey on the street in front of the house in winter, no matter what the temperature. Visits from the Martens family and all of the neighbourhood kids, made for play central at the van der Sloot house (hide and seek across the whole block, red rover, kick the can, etc.) It was a very active childhood. We loved riding our bikes in the open prairies behind the house. I was very close to 'Brownie', our little dog, that decided to come play with the children in the yard, nipping at our heels, and we could never let him go after that. Jim played the violin until Grade 10, when he became preoccupied with football, basketball and of course, girls. Of special interest was a cheerleader from Crescent Heights High (the competition high school) that was later to become his wife. At age of 17 and 18 he spent several months living away from home in California; once with Uncle Ron and once with two of his friends. After enjoyable rather than productive times in University of Calgary, he graduated with his Bachelor of Commerce in 1984 and articled for his CA designation with Coopers & Lybrand in Calgary until 1988. During that time he married his high school sweetheart, Sue Gross (June 7, 1986). In 1988 he joined forces with his Dad to acquire an accounting firm in Medicine Hat. Within one year of moving to Medicine Hat, Jim had gained his CA designation, become a partner and become a father for the first time; Jessica born December 7, 1989. The next few years were busy building his practice. During that time his son Nicholas was born (July 29, 1992). The kids grew up in a split level home on Cunliffe Crescent that, though drafty, was very much a home we will always remember. Dad retired and sold his practice to Calvin MacPhail and the business became van der Sloot, Anderson & MacPhail. Finally Calvin and Jim struck out on their own to form van der Sloot & MacPhail in 1996 (now Ensminger, Beck and Thomson). Jim became involved in oil and gas related businesses in 1997 and continued to work in that industry through several companies (Corlac, Enhanced Energy, Ensource, Strad, Alberta Petroleum Energy, Enerstar, and more).

TONY

I was born in Medicine Hat, Alberta, on May 25, 1963. I grew up in the 'Hat and graduated from McCoy High School in 1981. After high school, I studied Commerce at the University of Calgary, graduating in 1986. Soon after obtaining my degree, I left the prairies for the west coast and started working at Deloitte and Touche in Vancouver. In 1988, in a west side neighbourhood, I met my future wife, Janine Maureen Baisley. I worked at D&T for just over four years before taking a position at BC Hydro, where I worked for five years. On February 17, 1990, Janine and I were married at Our Lady of Perpetual Help, a small church in beautiful Point Grey where we were parishioners and close to where we first met. In 1996, Janine and I left Vancouver with our two and four year old and moved to Medicine Hat, where as a CPA, I have worked primarily in the oil and gas business. Janine and I have five beautiful children: John (1992),

Katherine (1994), Matthew (1997), William (1999), and Benjamin (2004).

PAUL

I was born on Valentine's Day in Medicine Hat, Alberta in 1965. While growing up in Medicine Hat I was active in a variety of sports including football, basketball, badminton and tennis. I was also heavily involved in music, playing the violin. In 1983, I graduated from McCoy High School and went on to study music at Brandon University in Manitoba and eventually graduated from the Eastman School of Music in 1987. While there, I met Patricia Pearman who I would marry in Great Falls, Virginia in 1989. I was co-director and co-founder of the Medicine Hat College Music Academy. I also freelanced and taught at Mount Royal Conservatory in Calgary. When we had our first child, Jennifer, in 1991 I made the decision to go back to school. I studied pre-med courses at the University of Calgary from 1991-93 while still teaching at Mount Royal College and subsequently was accepted to the School of Medicine at the University of Alberta. I completed my MD degree in 1997 and went on to complete a residency in otolaryngology (ENT) at the University of Alberta in 2002. While in Edmonton, Kathryn (1995), Thomas (1997) and Samuel (1999) were born. From there I went on to a fellowship in head and neck surgical oncology and microvascular reconstruction at Vanderbilt University in Nashville, Tennessee. In 2003, I took a faculty position at West Virginia University in Morgantown, West Virginia and stayed there until 2009 when we moved to Rochester, New York and I took a position at the University of Rochester where I continue to work. While working I completed a Master's in Business Management from the Simon School of Business at the University of Rochester. Patty and I have remained busy following our children through all their endeavors including cross country, track and wrestling. We have enjoyed every moment!

MARIANNE

Marianne was born on October 1, 1966, in Medicine Hat, and attended McCoy High School. Upon graduation in 1984, she attended the University of Lethbridge and the

University of Calgary, earning a B.Mus. in piano performance in 1989, and a B.Ed. in 1990. She met Leonard Bleile at the University of Calgary, and they were married on July 11, 1992. Marianne taught at St. Martha's and Father Damien Elementary School in Calgary, while Leonard was working as an electrical engineer at Northern Telecom. When their first child was born in 1995, Marianne quit working in the school, but she resumed teaching piano in 2004, and has worked as an accompanist for 35 years. Marianne homeschooled their two daughters, Sarah and Mary.

CAROLINE

I was born after the twins on Jan. 25, 1970 in Medicine Hat. Growing up I had the opportunity to figure skate, dance, and took violin, piano, voice and speech arts lessons. After graduation, I majored in violin performance for 2 years studying in Erlangen, Germany, as well as Mount Royal College and the University of Calgary. After that, I changed career paths and earned a Bachelor of Science in Nursing at the University of Alberta. I have worked for 20 years in the areas of Disability

Management, Occupational Nursing, Clinic Nursing, NICU, and Public Health. I married Jack Panteluk on Aug. 5, 1995 and we lived in Edmonton until 2002 when we moved to Red Deer, Alberta. We have 4 children - 2 boys and 2 girls. The boys were born in Edmonton and girls in Red Deer. Andrew was born in 1998, Luke in 2000, Julianna in 2002, and Veronica was born in 2004.

MARY JANE

Mary Jane Gerilynn was born in Medicine Hat on St. Gerard's Day, October 16th, 1971. Upon graduating from McCoy High school in 1989, Mary Jane moved to Rochester, New York to pursue an undergrad in violin performance. She went on to study both music and science and completed her BMUS at the University of British Columbia in violin performance. Mary Jane then played with the Vancouver Symphony Orchestra and at the same time was travelling abroad to Europe, Taiwan, the Caribbean Islands and Alaska with various groups through Cruise Lines and the Canadian Trade Commissioner. Mary Jane met Phil Vandekerkhove who was also studying at UBC in Finance. Phil and Mary Jane married at St. Patricks Church in Medicine Hat, AB July 19, 1997. Since then, they have had six wonderful children; Philip - 1997, Anthony - 2000, Dominic - 2001, Gerrilyn - 2007, Maria - 2010 and Clara - 2013, who is the youngest grandchild of Helen. Mary Jane is a stay at home mom and has also been teaching violin at the Mount Royal University Conservatory and performing within Calgary while Phil works as a Chartered Accountant in the oil and gas industry.

MICHAEL

Michael van der Sloot born July 1, 1974 married Daphne Boeda born July 6, 1975 in Calgary at St. Luke's Parish July 27, 1996. Michael and Daphne have 6 kids: Jacob Oct. 21, 1997, Anne May 21-2000, Sophie May 4 – 2002, Grace March 6 – 2006, Ambrose Dec. 14 – 2007, Josephine Jan. 11 – 2010. Michael grew up in Medicine Hat playing music and a variety of sports. Michael obtained a B.Mus. and M.Mus from the University of British Columbia and pursued graduate studies at the Mozarteum in Austria. Michael was instructor and Academy

Director at the Medicine Hat College for 11 years. Michael currently is Head of strings at the Victoria Conservatory of Music where he and Daphne enjoy a very full life!

Helen (left) and Lydia (right) in Germany.

Rose Siebert

Jakob Siebert

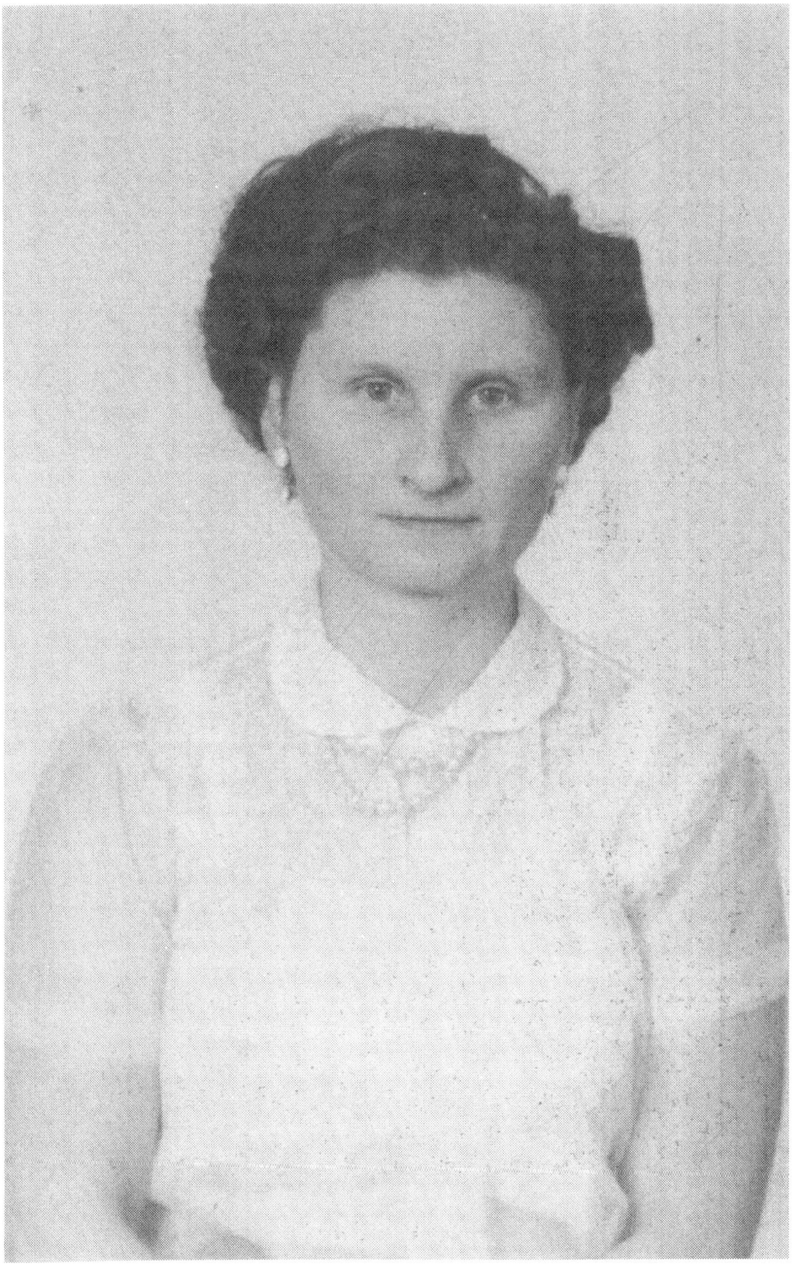

Rose Bauer

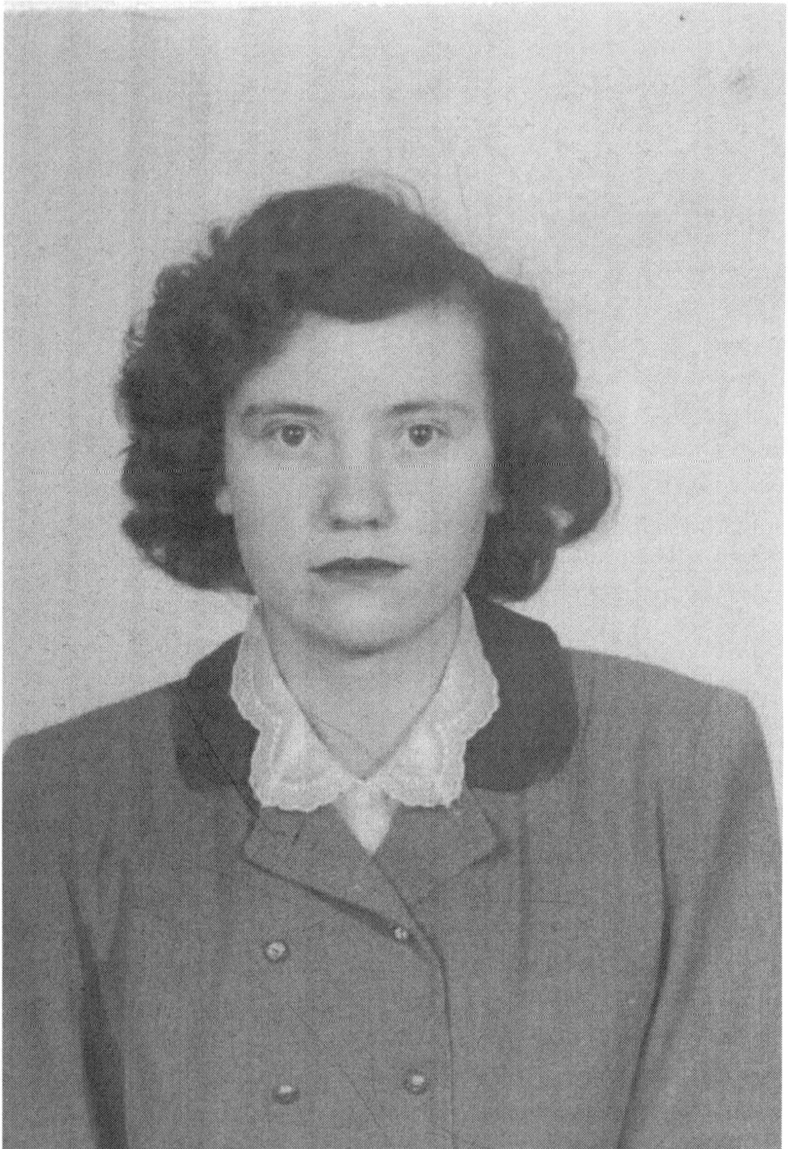

Lydia Siebert

Ron Siebert

Ron Siebert

Rose and Ron Siebert

Helen (left) and Rose (right) Siebert

Helen Siebert

Helen Siebert (left) and Rose Bauer (right)

Rose Bauer

Helen Siebert

Lydia Siebert

Ron Siebert

Helen Siebert

Lydia Siebert

Helen Siebert

Lydia Siebert

Lydia Siebert

Helen Siebert

Bert van der Sloot

Ron Siebert

Helen Siebert

Father Verhagen and Helen

Father Verhagen

Pete and Lydia's wedding.

Helen and Bert

Bert (left), Lydia (middle), and Pete (right) at Chief Mountain, Montana.

Ron (left), Helen (middle), and Bert (right) with children.

Bert (left), Helen (middle), and Lydia (right) at Bert and Helen's wedding.

Bert and Helen's wedding.

Helen feeding a deer.

Bert and Helen

Ron Siebert.

Ron and Lucy.

Rose Siebert (left), Rose Bauer (middle), and Jakob Siebert (right)

Helen and Bert with children.

The Memoirs of Ron Siebert

Forward

This autobiography is the story of myself, Ron (Reinhard)* Siebert; beginning with my parents- Jakob and Rosa Siebert. The reason for not going back further chronologically, is simply that very little is known of my forebears beyond grandparents, uncles and aunts of whom only eight are remembered and known to me personally. I have tried to be as accurate as possible, relying totally on word-of-mouth accounts from Mother, Father, and sisters and personal experiences from my very early youth to the present. I regret that the importance of family history did not occur to me until well into midlife and towards the end of Mom and Dad's lives, by which time their memories had dimmed considerably. Consequently, some important events may have been diminished or even missed. I would be remiss if I did not acknowledge the contribution of timely and important details by my sisters, Helen and Lydia. Finally, I dedicate this effort to the memory of Mother, Father, and sister Rosa whose wisdom and patience have guided me in this life journey. My admiration for their compassion, love, patience, dedication to human decency, and hard work in raising the family despite unbelievably daunting hardships and challenges- is everlasting. Never has any generation suffered as they did, but in spite of all that, managed to overcome adversity to provide us children the opportunity and environment to thrive and fulfill our own life's ambitions. My respect grows daily as does my gratitude for all the sacrifices they made for the family. May God bless and keep you and reward you abundantly. I miss you.

*Please note my first name is Reinhard in parenthesis: this is my official (German) name given me by my parents at birth, but in practice used only by my immediate family (parents/sisters)- thus all further references to me will be my preferred name, Ron.

Dedication

I dedicate this autobiography to my wife Lucy, whose constant encouragement and constant reminders to tell my story for the sake of our children, patiently made this effort possible. As everyone knows, I rarely spoke about my early years, because quite frankly they are somewhat painful. By not talking about it, a form of self-denial, I took comfort in believing it never happened. In retrospect, however, I came to realize that hardships, deprivation, pain, and suffering (both physical and emotional) strengthen and build character thereby generating a will power and a determination necessary to surmount obstacles and challenges later in life. So, dear Lucy, on the occasion of our 40th wedding anniversary, this is my story!

I was born on January 2, 1938, in Neu-Lebental, Ukraine; the youngest of four children and the only son of Jakob and Rosa Siebert. My oldest sister, Rose, was a half sister from my mother's first marriage. My two other sisters, Helen and Lydia, were born on January 14, 1933 and August 16, 1934, respectively and also in Neu-Lebental.

Before delving into my own story, it is imperative and important for the greater benefit, that I explore my parents' background. My parents are part of a generation that has been called with no exaggeration "The Greatest Generation", and not without merit. Consider in general what they survived- prosperity, revolution, famine, two World Wars, and a Depression. It makes you wonder how they managed to suffer through these calamities and still come out of it decent, God-fearing, and law-abiding citizens. With this in mind, let me explore my parents' background, starting with mom.

My mother was born on August 16, 1898, in the Ukraine. She was the child of Adam Zoeller, my grandfather, and Emilie Moor, my grandmother. Both my parents and grandparents were of German descent and very proud of it. They spoke very little Russian (Ukrainian) and what little schooling they had was all in German. This raised an obvious question to me- why didn't they speak Russian or consider themselves Russian? The answer was quite simple. During the reign of Empress Catharine of Russia (she was German) in the year 1763 she issued a manifesto enticing West Europeans to settle in her country. She needed to bolster her population with strong, hard-working people. She promised much to the new settlers: freedom of religion, freedom from taxes for a five to thirty year period, freedom from military service and generous allotments of free land to farmers. This was a very attractive proposition and many settlers came including scores from central and southern Germany. And so it was that small German settlements were established, mainly in the Ukraine, the "Bread Basket" of Russia. With that bit of background information let's go back to mother's resume.

There were 11 children, 3 boys and 8 girls. The family lived on a large farm, the exact size of which I have no idea.

Farm life in those days was very demanding and time consuming considering that all land cultivation was accomplished by horses and oxen drawn equipment. Thus, the days began at sunrise and continued until sunset. The men in the family would feed and tend to the needs of the animals, i.e. groom and clean the horses, milk and feed the cows, clean the barn, and feed all other animals i.e. calves, chickens, hogs, and dogs, etc. They would then come in for a hearty and healthy breakfast. My mother loved to tell us how my grandfather would always start his day with a straight shot of whiskey, exclaiming it was good for the health. When mother spoke of her father- her love, respect, and admiration were self-evident. She spoke of how generous and helpful he was to anyone falling in need. He expected his children to do the same. Along with his compassion for others, my mother often told of how hard he and her brothers worked in the fields and how well he treated and cared for the animals, especially the horses. They knew him very well and neighed when they saw him coming. At the end of a long and tiring day, before the men cleaned up to eat, the horses were cleaned, groomed, and fed. Then, but not before, the family would sit down to eat.

Mom told many stories about her brothers and sisters. Basically, they were all hard-working, God-fearing people. One story my mother liked to tell was the time her oldest brother 'John' raced his horse too hard. A favorite pastime of the young guys was to race their horses (today it's cars) against each other. Well, according to mother, John was a bit of a hellion and one day he raced his horse too hard and when he came home Grandfather noticed how sweaty, lathered up, and dirty the pony was. Grandfather was very angry with John. To make a long story short, John ended up cleaning, grooming, and feeding the horse and was forbidden to mount that horse (a beauty according to mother) for several weeks. The lesson here was that all horses were to be cared for and not abused since without strong, healthy horses, farming was impossible. Because of her father's devotion and love of horses, mother too knew and loved horses and could never walk past one without petting and remarking on its beauty! They were her weakness. She knew all about horses because of Grandfather. Needless to say, it rubbed off on me.

As far as the women of the house were concerned, they too worked from sunrise to sunset. Mom told of getting up well before sunrise and lighting and fueling the stove to heat water and cook breakfast. She reminded us that there was no power or gas in those days, in fact even coal was scarce so that their fires were fed by straw, wood, and even dried manure. Thus it required constant attention. While minding the fire, mother would pray and study her catechism before school. Practicing their Catholic faith was as much a way of life as was working. Mother only had about three years of school- just enough to read, write, and do a little arithmetic. Bear in mind, in those days education was not considered essential. In fact, most if not all, considered it secondary to farming. Mother always spoke well of her parents and brothers and sisters. Grandfather was well respected in the community (served as mayor) and was always approached and consulted- valued for help and advice. Grandmother was just a sincerely decent and generous human being that always helped the poor and ministered to the sick. Grandmother was a quiet person; slender in stature and very intelligent. Mother always spoke highly of all her brothers and sisters, and you could tell she cared for and loved them all very, very much.

In time, mother was an exact facsimile of her parents and siblings. To sum up, she was always kind, generous and compassionate with a strong work ethic and just as strong religious convictions. One can only hope that at least a smidgen of that decency rubbed off on yours truly.

As for father, he was born in Konteniusfeld, Ukraine, on February 14, 1907, the 4th child of Jakob, my grandfather and Helen, my grandmother. As was the case with mother, he was raised in a German community where German prevailed. Father too was raised on a farm under much the same living conditions that prevailed in mother's community, with one big difference- father's community was Mennonite, which is a Protestant denomination. This difference created some problems in later years. Father's life on the farm differed in one respect from boys his own age. He liked school and early on decided he wanted to be a teacher. In a farm family such as his, this was heresy and totally at odds with mores of the times. Remember, in those days, education was secondary and boys were expected and very much needed to work the farm. But father was determined to become a teacher and so after finishing school locally he approached and apprised his father (my grandfather) of his dream. His father was very upset and told father that his place was on the farm with the rest of the family. Father persisted and finally my grandfather relented, but he would not support the cost of studying elsewhere except for a minor sum that he gave to dad on his departure. Thus, with not a little bitterness, father left the warmth of his home and family, to study in a strange, far off place with very little money and no means of support other than some minor stipends from the Government. Somehow he managed to scrape up the money to support himself as he pursued his dream of becoming a teacher. What determination! What sacrifice! In spite of his meager finances, father would proudly tell me of how fellow students at college would comment about his neat appearance. He could afford only cheap clothes and wore then until they were threadbare. He explained it this way to me: "You don't have to have the latest or most expensive clothes on the market, just be sure they fit well and keep them neat and clean." This neatness and tidiness lasted a lifetime as anyone who ever saw his clothes closet, garage, yard, or car can testify. Everything was in its place- "neat and clean". In the end, father became a teacher, getting his first assignment in the town my mother lived in- Neu-Lebental.

It is here, as you've guessed by now, that father met mother and the rest is history. Before I begin my story, it behooves me to set the stage, by a brief description of the social and political climate of the times prior to my parents' wedding. Bear in mind the great upheaval caused by the Bolshevik Revolution of 1917. Profound changes took place in the Soviet Union that made a dramatic impact on the lifestyle of my family.

Well-to-do farmers and/or business people were declared Gulaks (an unflattering description) and their land and property were confiscated and placed in communes. Thus, destroying pride in ownership. Both my families experienced this upheaval. Next, Communist thugs forcibly abducted these Gulaks and their adult sons in the middle of the night, almost never to be seen again. I say 'almost never' because some did return, half-dead, a shell of their former self. Speculation has it that a few were allowed to return to live as an example of what happens to dissidents and to intimidate the populace. Churches were closed to religious service, and re-opened to become theatres or dance halls. Schools were strictly prohibited from any religious teaching or activity and curricula changed to advance the Communist ideology. People were encouraged to inform on each other and/or their family. Kangaroo courts run by Communist thugs conducted slow trials on any pretext to weed out anyone suspected of anti-communist activities. Distrust of your fellow citizen and neighbor was encouraged. In short, what was once a happy way of life turned into a real hell. And in the late 1920's a family, intentionally created by the Communist Regime (Stalin), wiped out nearly half the population. My parents and their families did not escape and many died of starvation. Many villagers came begging and my mother's family would always share what little they had. Once a lady came and saw their little dog and begged to have it because they could make some soup and it would keep them from starving. She took the dog home and later informed my grandmother how good it was. However, later the lady also died of starvation. What saved the life of many people was the "American Kitchen". The USA sent sacks of flour, grain, etc. to feed the starving people. My mother's stories about how they survived and in what especially is too painful to relate. Let it suffice to say they were survivors, but let me remind you that it was in this climate of mistrust, turmoil, and uncertainty that my parents had the courage to marry and raise a family in the hope of a better future. This remained their fervent wish until they died.

Hopefully, with this very abbreviated and general background of their individual lives, I finally come to the point in their lives when their paths crossed, culminating in union through marriage. As stated earlier, in 1929, father received his first assignment as a teacher in Neu-Lebental, home of my mother and her family. He took up room and board at my grandparents' home, because as mentioned earlier, they were always first to assist people even if they were strangers. In the case of father, they were in large part responsible for his assignment to their village. So it was at my grandparents' home that that father met mother. Mother was eight and a half years older than father and was a single parent at this time, with a seven year old daughter (sister Rose). Her first husband had died at a very early age of diphtheria/typhoid, a disease that had killed many, many people.

And so mother was left with the small family farm that the Communists had allowed each renter. Mother was overwhelmed at first- how could she, a woman, perform the myriad and time-consuming chores that farming in these days demanded. Even in retellings of the story, her eyes would well up.

But, not to worry, here again, her family came to the rescue. When it came to the very hard work of cultivating, planting, and harvesting, grandfather's edict to the family (all her brothers and sisters, married or single) was Rose's came first. Then in early spring, her crops were planted first and in fall they were, again, the first to be harvested. Mother was always touched by her family's total support. She knew she was taken care of.

Now, it was in this setting that father met mother. Father liked mom from the beginning; her kindness, her looks, and her general bearing and conduct. Mother too, liked father, but she felt intimidated by him, because he was an educated man, looked up to by her family and the community. Remember, as stated earlier, farming was always of primary concern in those days; nonetheless, educated people were highly regarded and respected. Add to this the fact she was married with a child and one can understand that in her mind the odds were against her. Yet they did fall in love and got married on January 31, 1932. The story of their wedding is worth telling. They were married at St. Mary's Church in Mannheim, Ukraine, by father Waliser (thanks to my sister, Helen). Only one other person, a witness, was present. Let me remind you that priests were forbidden by the Communist Regime to say Mass or administer the Sacraments. So my parents were married in secret with no friends or relatives present and after, no celebrating, so as not to alert the authorities. After the wedding, they took a train from Mannheim to Raduschna where they arrived at 11:00 pm. They had a six mile walk to Neu-Lebental (home) in bitter cold. On the way, they got lost and when they eventually got home, grandmother awaited them with a lit candle, a little glass of wine and a little food. And so began the married life of mother and father. What a honeymoon!

And there you have, regretfully, a meager description of all I know of my family history prior to mother and father. It is fervently hoped that this will serve as a benchmark for the beginning of a Siebert Family Tree. Hopefully, those who follow will keep it current and growing! With this in mind, my story follows.

I was born in Neu-Lebental on January 2, 1938, the third of three children and the only boy. A third sister (Rose) came from Mom's prior marriage. The village of Neu-Lebental was a German settlement within the province of Dnepropetrowsk, Ukraine. The nearest city of size was Krivojrog. As told earlier, in my brief resume of Mom and Dad, all aspects and transactions of everyday life were conducted in German i.e. church, school, business, etc. Church or any religious services were held clandestinely, as was mom and dad's marriage. The penalty if caught practicing or teaching religion was severe. Another example of the severity of breaking the Communist edict against religion or its practice proves the point. As told earlier, dad was a teacher and he started every school day with a prayer. And although the village was a close knit community with time-honored traditions of mutual trust and respect, in time this was eroded by Communist propaganda via a coercive measure such as encouraging people to inform against each other (brother against brother was actually ordered) and pervaded the community. And so it was that someone out of spite or jealousy reported dad to the authorities. Dad was duly tried on charges of practicing religion illegally. Dad was immediately dismissed from his teaching position and had it not been for the intercession of the townspeople on his behalf, a fate much worse could have befallen him. (This happened in 1936.) Another incident depicting the pervasive atmosphere of distrust and fear, will help the reader understand the culture of intimidation that existed at this time- an atmosphere that was fostered by, encouraged, and rewarded by the local Communist thugs.

This next incident occurred a year or two after dad had been relieved of his teaching position. Subsequent to his firing, dad had taken courses in bookkeeping, which resulted in his appointment as bookkeeper of the local commune. By way of a short explanation- a Communist commune was centralized enterprise that was totally owned and operated according to the dictates of the Central Communist Party in Moscow. Thus, any land or shop, any commercial endeavor whatever, was the property of the state, not the individual. Except for a house, a garden, a cow, a pig, and four children- everything belonged to the state and supposedly the proceeds of the community were distributed equally to all members of the commune after the Party had taken its share- which was the bulk. But as history has proven, folks produced more in their private gardens and plots than did the gigantic communes, and again producing the superiority of pride of individual ownership vs. communal ownership.

Getting back to dad's predicament as bookkeeper of the commune, it was practice at the end of the harvest, that whatever was left after the Party's take, was distributed to village people. Again, someone out of spite or coercion accused dad of basically doctoring the books to provide more of the harvest to the people. Again, dad was put on trial and could have been sentenced to jail and/or exiled to the cold north (Siberia) to slave in mines, never to return. However, due to the intercession of fellow workers and citizens, dad was absolved. But the fear and loathing of Communist thugs was ever present and the family lived in constant fear, not only from the Communist Party, but also its informers, which by the time (late '30's and early '40's) had totally infiltrated the populace of not only Moscow and the large urban cities, but had drifted down to the rural towns and villages including Neu-Lebental.

A final episode will illustrate the dismal state of everyday life during my very early life (1938-1943). Not only had the Communists sown the seed of distrust and envy among its citizens in every corner of the Soviet Union, but it suppressed violently and brutally any insurrection or opposition real or imagined. Surprisingly, some small bands of guerillas still existed and operated clandestinely at this time (remember, the Communist Revolution occurred in 1917). And so it was that one night a snowstorm was raging outside, my parents were awakened by a knock on the door. Both mom and dad sweated bullets, because the Communists were notorious for breaking into homes during the night and abducting the head of the house for trumped up charges and exiling them to Siberia to work in slave camps or mines until they were worked to death or so near that they became useless. A few starved, and near death, were allowed to return home to serve as examples to the local infidels. So it is understandable, the agonizing fear experienced by mom and dad by the knock on the door. When they opened the door, to their surprise and relief, it was not a Party cache, but a haggard and half-starved stranger. He pleaded for food and bed until morning, when he would leave before dawn. You can imagine the anxiety and fear this elicited from mom and dad. If they were caught harboring a dissident, their punishment would be severe. However, their compassion overcame fear and they fed and sheltered the man for a few hours. While ravenously eating his fod, dad conversed with the man, learning that he was a very well-educated man, totally opposed to Communist dogma and part of a group of dissidents who actively opposed the Communists by using guerilla tactics of sabotage as well as distributing pieces of secret dissident literature. After his meal, this stranger wrote a nice poem in appreciation of my parent's assistance.

It was by sheer accident that the poem landed in my sister, Rose's schoolbook. Several days later while using the book during a class, a teacher happened to see the poem. Said teacher (Mr. Quirring) took the poem and for whatever reason, possibly to endear himself to the authorities, delivered the poem to them. This was serious stuff that went beyond the confines of our little town. In due course, dad was charged with harboring a fugitive and ordered to appear at a court hearing in the district headquarter city of Dnepropetrowks. Everyone thought dad was a goner. Mom was beside herself. She was sure we would never see dad again and it was indeed a sad, sad farewell when dad was escorted to his hearing.

At the hearing, when dad was allowed to speak, his defense was a simple question. He told the tribunal (Kangaroo Court) that he felt this man was a poor traveling man, who was exhausted and hungry and who needed help. Naturally, dad did not acknowledge the fact that he knew the man was a guerrilla. He then asked "If this man had come to your house, would you not have done as we did?" Subsequently, dad was sent to Kiev and Moscow for more interrogations. Fortunately for us, we had a boarder at our home. He was working for the Communists; but was a good-hearted man. He might have been a Communist outwardly, but deep in his heart he was not. He spoke well on behalf of my dad, and it was because of him and God's merciful intervention (mom always said), that dad was not sent to Siberia. The case was dismissed and dad was able to return to a jubilant family.

This unfortunately is not the end of this incident however. During the course of the hearing, for whatever reason, the prosecutor presented, in chains, the poor man we had harbored. Dad and the man recognized each other immediately, but dad felt like he had been stabbed through the heart, for in that moment, it occurred to dad, that the poor devil probably thought that dad was the informer that resulted in his capture and incarcerating and most likely his death. Since there was no way dad could talk to the prisoner, the fact dogged dad for the rest of his life. Every time dad told this story, you could feel his pain- he would always say "that poor guy probably blamed me for his capture."

As I said, this pained dad and the rest of the family. So there you have final example of the horrible conditions that existed during my first five years of life. Fortunately for me, I was too young to understand the tragedy of those early years. Only after reaching the age of maturity did the horror and pain of these stories really sink in. Because of this, remembrances of Neu-Lebental are only positive and happy ones as they would be for any child under the age of five years.

So then, what do I remember of my home and family while living in Neu-Lebental, the village of my birth? To begin with, I was born not in a hospital, but in our home, under the caring eye of my grandmother, who served as mid-wife and doctor. This was normal for that time and that way of life. Naturally, (I'm told) this was a happy occasion, especially since I was the first and only boy in the family. My remembrances of family and home are only happy ones, as you would expect from a child.

Our house was what nowadays would probably be an average two or three bedroom home. There was a living room, but the kitchen was the center of activity. It's where we lived! The house was built of straw and mud, and the roof was covered by thatch- a material stronger and longer lasting than straw. The mud I speak of was actually a mixture of mud (clay) and straw which was first formed into bricks, which after curing, were used to build the walls. Very little, if any, lumber was used, and this was probably due to the lack of trees (forest) in that region. The only trees I remember were a couple of cherry trees in our backyard, but the countryside was void of any trees and I suspect this was a prairie-like region.

I heard my parents often speak of the hard work involved in building the home. It began of course with the making of the mud bricks, which involved mixing mud with straw. This was accomplished by digging up dirt (which apparently was heavy duty clay), adding water and straw, then stomping on the mix with bare feet in order to get a good homogenous mixture, which was then put into molds to form bricks. After duly drying in the sun, the bricks were removed from the molds and made ready for use in the building of the home. As stated earlier, the roof was made of a heavy straw or thatch, which needless to say, must have been a constant fire hazard and had to be frequently repaired to stop or prevent leaks.

Humble? Yes- but still a home and as good as any available at that time. Was it cold in the winter- you bet! Bear in mind, this was cold country in the northern latitudes. Winters lasted seven to eight months a year and ice and snow covered the yard for about the whole winter. The house was kept warm by an oven located in the kitchen and was fueled only during the day by straw and coal and dung. This oven or stove also served our cooking needs. I remember it well- for I once fell in such a way that my head was lodged between a wall and the stove. Mom pulled me out but not before I was severely burned on one side of my face. But other than that burn, I only remember one other painful experience. That episode involved a sewing machine.

In those days, every housewife, among a myriad of chores, had to be a seamstress as well. My mother was a good one. She owned a hand-driven sewing machine and on this machine sewed and repaired just about all the clothes the family needed. Apparently, I had a real fascination for the sewing machine and would sit and watch mother use it. One time, for whatever reason, I managed to get one of my fingers too close to the needle and the needle penetrated right through my finger, including the fingernail. My mother remembered all this very vividly and it still made her queasy, especially when it came to the part where she had to extract the needle. Needless to say, I stayed away from that sewing machine after that.

In addition to the house itself, every home had a barn attached to it. The barn housed a cow, a horse or two, a pig, several chickens, mules, and a sheep or two. The livestock was essential for our sustenance, providing us with dairy and meat products and even leather and wool. Additionally, we had a good-sized garden which provided us with vegetables the whole year round. There were no refrigerators and meats were stored in barrels, liberally covered with salt to preserve them. Both meats and vegetable were stored in root cellars for preservation until they we consumed or until they were replenished by the next harvest or butchering. Then every home was self-sufficient in dairy products and produce, thanks to their garden. Cereal products (flour, sugar, oatmeal, etc.) were doled out by the commissioners from the communal farm, in exchange for long hours of labor put in by every household. Most of the communal harvest was shipped out to wherever the Central Party wanted it shipped. A meager portion was doled out to the village. Thus as stated earlier, the bulk of foodstuffs per household came from privately owned gardens and livestock.

As a hobby, father had a single beehive. More than a hobby, however, he would use fresh honey and honeycomb for bartering; i.e. 'x' pounds of honey for a side of beef or pork. You can't believe how good the honeycomb used to be- like candy- of which there was very little. On the other hand, I do recall being stung by bees, more than once. Mother tells of an incident where a neighboring boy while poking a stick into the hive, was attacked and severely stung by the bees. My parents were extremely worried about a reoccurrence and subsequently built a strong fence around the hive to prevent other children from bothering the bees.

Thus my early childhood was a happy, carefree time. Any shortages or problems due to the political machinations of the time were beyond my comprehension and so my memories of that time are pleasant indeed. All the hardships of the times were overshadowed by the caring and loving presence of good friends and the extended families. I vaguely remember some aunts and my grandmother, all of whom treated me as if I were their very own. Grandmother was nothing but kindness. She always had something for me, in spite of the meager times. As for my aunts, I remember especially Aunt Lisa (mother's younger sister). They lived at the other end of the village where we would visit and I would play with a cousin (name forgotten) while the adults visited. One especially memorable visit involved a watermelon from Aunt Lisa's garden. I don't recall who accompanied me to Aunt Lisa's, except for some unexplainable reason I found myself alone in her garden. And there in front of me was the largest watermelon I had ever seen in my life. By this time, I knew how good watermelon tasted and I decided I would please the family by bringing it home. The idea of taking it without anyone's permission never occurred to me. So I took that watermelon and lugged it home, dropping it numerous times along the way. By the time I got it home, it had quite a few cracks and bruises, but I made it. In the process, I dirtied my pants BIG TIME. But so what! But so what? Pleasing mother, I thought, would make it all worthwhile. Well to my surprise, mother was not at all pleased and sternly demanded to know where I got it, who gave it to me, etc.! So, I told her Aunt Lisa gave it to me. Well, unfortunately for me, she didn't buy that at all and threatened to go confront Aunt Lisa immediately. This could be trouble I knew, because I never asked or talked to Aunt Lisa about any watermelon. I just took it. About this time, father entered the house and of course mother had to tell him the whole story. You can imagine how as a four or five year old I was sweating bullets. I don't know whatever happened except that I saw mom and dad exchanging winks and I thought I saw a bit of a smirk on dad's face. The last thing I remember was my mother taking off my clothes and cleaning me up, not too gently I should add.

Several other events come to mind during the early life and I mention them only to illustrate the living conditions at the time. For example, there was no running water and no inside plumbing. We got our water from a well in the yard. I remember that well very well because I was always told that a boogey-man lived inside that well and that the creature loved to grab little boys and pull them down into the well. The idea of course was to keep me away from the well and possibly falling into it. Needless to say, it worked. I always gave that well a wide berth.

As far as plumbing, I know there was nothing inside the house. So we obviously would have done our thing either outside or in the barn with the animals. Either way, it all ended up as fertilizer in the garden, or as fuel for the oven as described earlier. It was all very primitive by today's standards. In fact, it was probably primitive even in those times when compared to Western European countries such as France, Germany, or Great Britain. Communism (the great equalizer) had managed to create an egalitarian state, but at the expense of modernization which kept the masses not only backward, but totally subservient. My parents and most of the population of the village had a strong affinity for Germany, being descendants of that heritage and consequently wanted to get out of Russia (Ukraine) in the worst way. Nobody dared express that view to the Party Commissioner for fear of being declared traitors and exile to Siberia where they worked and starved to death. Then when Germany invaded Russia, there was a secret joy in the

German community. They were regarded as saviors. Bear in mind, both parents had come from well-to-do, hard-working families where hard work was rewarded by the good life (by standards of the time). All that had been taken away by the Communists so one can understand their bitterness toward the Communists. Add to this the fact that as Germans, they were always under a cloud of suspicion whenever breaches of security or acts of sabotage occurred. Thus the years from 1941 to 1943 were a time of great stress and fear for the German community. With that in mind, I now turn to a great turning point in the life of my family.

As mentioned earlier, the Germans invaded Russia in August 1941 and by 1943 had reached as far as Stalingrad (St. Petersburg nowadays). Thus, Neu-Lebental too was occupied by the Germans. The inhabitants actually welcomed the Germans with open arms and actually viewed them as liberating heroes. The Germans immediately started breaking up the communes and privatizing land, livestock, equipment, etc., to the joy of the people. This state of affairs didn't last long however (sorry I can't give you dates) as the Germans met ferocious resistance in Stalingrad that actually stalled, then reversed the German invasion and soon the Germans actually found themselves in retreat in the fall of 1943.

Now during their brief stay in Neu-Lebental, some German soldiers were billeted in private homes. And so it was that we had a young officer staying with us who was involved in administering the village. The whole family took a liking to him. He spent a lot of time playing with me and brought me toys and goods. He was like family. There were good times, but the tide of war was turning and the Soviets went on the offensive. Nightly you could see the sky light up and hear the thunder of artillery in the distance. Everyone was weary if not outright scared, but the Germans always reassured the people that the tide would again turn in their favor. But it never did, and finally the front approached so close that the order to evacuate was issued by the Germans. Under German auspices all of those of German origin were given the option of remaining, or retreating with the Germans to eventually end up in Germany. To my knowledge, all but a few in our village chose to evacuate even though it meant giving up everything that they owned, not to mention leaving their home and way of life. And so our family prepared to leave everything that was close to their heart. Meager though it was- it was home, it was extended family and friends. And so begins the saga of my family's exodus from the village of my birth.

On October 20, 1943, a day after being ordered to evacuate within 24 hours by the Germans, we waved good-bye to our home and joined a wagon train, expecting to reach freedom in Germany within a couple of weeks. No one had any idea of the nightmares that were to befall us. And so it was a bittersweet day. Many tears flowed on leaving our home, but that was tempered by the joy of embarking on a journey to freedom. For me, being only five years old, the prospect of living and sleeping in a wagon was exciting. I had no concept of the hardships and pain and suffering such an adventure would inflict on both man and heart. And so we joined a wagon train that extended as far as the eye could see. Our covered wagon was drawn by four horses which were taken from the Kolchos (communal farm). We loaded the wagon with food, warm clothes, bedding, and fodder for the horses. I recall the loading of the wagon vividly. Remember, only one day was allowed for planning and packing. So there was a lot of frantic activity involving butchering livestock, choosing clothes, bedding and all the belongings of a normal household. Over and over choices had to be made between items dear to someone's heart vs. items of necessity to sustain life. The choice was clear and the bulk of our belongings were left behind. The wagon was loaded to capacity with pots, pans, stove and sundry other gadgets hanging on the side and a cow in tow. Just like you see in western movies except this was real.

The wagon-trek began on a clear and warm day. Both man and beast were in good shape physically, if not spiritually or emotionally. We were escorted and protected by German soldiers. We traveled mainly on unpaved side roads, so as not to interfere or impede the German army which was in retreat. Artillery and gunfire were a constant presence. But the first few days went well and were actually exciting to me as I recall skipping and playing alongside the wagon until I got tired, when I would jump on the wagon and rest or sleep.

We covered about 30 km per day and at night would stay at communes for the night. Fodder for the horses was taken forcefully from the commune by the German escorts. I should explain that the wagon train consisted of a number of villages, but each village tried to stay together both during travel and at rest, so as to maintain its own identity as well as order.

We were part of this wagon train for six weeks and it soon became a nightmare, even for me, who had enjoyed the first couple of days. Bear in mind, all during this six-week period there was actual war waging between Russian and German armies. Thus there were bombing, strafing, and raids directed at each other without any regard for wagon trains such as ours. Additionally, there was guerrilla action by Russians, aimed primarily at the German army, but at our wagon train as well. The Russians hated Germans and did not discriminate between army or civilian in their effort to punish the invader. The civilians were considered traitors and saboteurs to their cause and quite probably not without cause. This was payback time for earlier defeats and losses at the hands of the Germans.

In addition to the problem of the military action, we encountered illness, cold, infestation of lice, and filthy living conditions. Getting stuck in the mud to our axels and broken wagons were tremendous obstacles. Lice, cold, and filthy conditions became a way of life! I recall not being able to sleep and crying because I was being eaten alive- head to toe, by lice and fleas. I don't recall ever being bathed and food, which was cooked over a campfire, was half raw and half rotten. Sanitary conditions were horrific; because there was no privacy. At night, together with strangers we slept in barns on straw or hay, with wind and at times snow or rain howling through cracks in the barn. So, if the lice didn't get you, the cold, snow, or rain would. Life became absolutely miserable. Everyone was sick or irritable. Human dignity took a beating and only because of German supervision some real tragedies were averted. Under such harsh circumstances peoples' civil manners deteriorated rapidly.

It was about this time in our journey, that we met Uncle Abraham, my dad's brother, who was married to a Ukrainian wife Lena. They lived here (name forgotten) with their little son, Eduard. Uncle Abraham was the only relative from my dad's side that we had ever seen, because before he was married, he came a few times to visit us in Neu-Lebental. We children loved him very much and always looked forward to his visits, and always had a lot of fun with him. He, too, had become a teacher. So it was that we met his wife (a wonderful lady) and our cousin, Eduard, for the first time. They invited us to stay overnight in their home, which was a real treat for us. Uncle Abraham and his family never left the Ukraine. We never saw them again. However, while living in Canada, we were able to find their whereabouts through the Red Cross, and so were able to stay in touch by correspondence.

As we fled by horse and buggy, babies were born on the way, but not all of them survived. The trip was very difficult for the elderly and some people fell ill. This happened to my sister Helen's friend's sister who became so sick that she had to be admitted to a hospital. The parents were given the assurance that the child would be re-united with the family after the child's recover. Unfortunately, this never happened. As time went on the father was recruited into the German army while the family lived in Poland. Later the mother and their three other children were sent to Siberia. Several years after the war, again through the Red Cross, they learned that their father was in Germany, and the daughter who had been in the hospital was married to a French man and lived in France. At that time the Russians did not allow the Germans to move to or even to visit in German. So, it happened that although the father did visit his daughter in France, he was not able to see the rest of his family. He would have been considered a traitor and had he returned to Russia, the Russians would have killed him. Eventually when the family was allowed to move to Germany, their dad had died. This is only one example of the dreadful events during the war and during the Communist times.

After six weeks with the wagon train (early December 1943) our wagon broke down hopelessly and our horses were spent with no shoes and with legs that were bleeding and so our family left the wagon train. The Germans had a military outpost in a place called Daraschnja, where they offered Dad a job as an interpreter until arrangements could be made for our evacuation. Thus after losing our home and then suffering horrendous hardships for six weeks, we lost our family and village people, never again to see most of them. This was a terrible blow, and yet a blessing in disguise, as very few of our village people ever made it to Germany.

We stayed in Daraschnja about five weeks. It was a fearful period as we were the only German family living in the confines of a Russian community that was hostile and bitter and bent on meting out revenge on any German or German sympathizer. Bear in mind that having their homeland invaded in brutal fashion was humiliating and degrading and their hatred for Germans or anything resembling Germany was understandable. Worse than reprisals from civilians, however, were reprisals meted out by Russian guerrillas, which hounded the German army with small but devastatingly effective attacks and skirmishes at places and times of their choosing. Thus mother told us of sleepless nights, when every footstep outside the house was a potential threat to the family. Firefights erupted nightly and we would not relax and sleep until the footsteps and disturbances receded into the night. Thus we lived- no, subsisted- for about five weeks, when the Germans determined that this place was too dangerous for a family and that they were unable to provide for our safety and security. Additionally, at this time the German military front was collapsing and the army was in full retreat.

And so towards the end of January 1944, the Germans put us and what few belongings we had on a truck and moved us west to a town called Gorodok in the Ukraine. Understand that this was not a nice little trip from one destination to another, but a harrowing experience, due to the guerilla harassment and always the bitter, bitter cold that we endured. Our stay in Gorodok was uneventful and short and served mainly as a gathering point for hoards of refugees such as ourselves and for us as a transfer point from truck to cattle train. This cattle train, which lasted about one full day and night was by majority opinion perhaps the worst disaster we had as yet experienced. Imagine the scene- middle of winter, people and their baggage rightly squeezed into unheated cattle cars, with no plumbing, no heat, no seats, and no food. For at least 24 hours- imagine the crying, cursing, screaming, and suffering in extremely tight quarters. It was an unforgettable nightmare with people urinating, defecating, and freezing to death in some cases.

The cattle train took us to Litzmannstadt which I believe was in Sudentland, Poland, and inhabited by people of German heritage, hence the German name. Even though we stayed in Litzmannstadt for only a couple of days, it was in my opinion a milestone or in the least a turning point in our journey. After the preceding 24-hour ordeal on the train, we were what I call transformed from basic animal instincts into human beings. Imagine, if you will, our condition: we hadn't bathed or even washed for days, we had been infested by lice for what seemed forever; all clothes were filthy; we had almost frozen and were subjected to inhuman hardships. So, here we are in

Litzmannstadt being cared for by a German women's organization. (In Germany, NSV or *Nationaler Sozialisten Verein* or National Socialist Union.) And we were no longer a single family trying to survive, but part of a refugee camp, totally dependent on every aspect of our livelihoods on strangers. We lived at, or because of, their mercy. So these strangers provided warmth, food, and medical treatment.

After that they proceeded to delouse and clean us. This was no small task. Women and children were stripped, and then showered together in a large shower room. Then their hair was washed with special solvents or shampoos to kill lice and other insects. Why do I mention this? Simply, because you cannot imagine how good it felt to be clean and free of lice. Remember, we had been infested by lice and tormented by them for what seemed like forever. They were everywhere but especially in your hair. The itching was unbearable and the constant scratching led to bleeding, open and infected sores. And so to be clean and free from the infernal itching was pure joy. We would never again suffer at the hands of those maddening parasites. In addition to the delousing, what clothes and/or belongings we had were processed through high temperature ovens to eradicate the lice forever. All in all, the short stopover in Litzmannstadt turned out to be a much needed respite from misery.

From Litzmannstadt we (the refugee camp) were transported by train to Freihermersdorf (Sudentland) for approximately four weeks. Here, we billeted in a school. A number of people including men, women, and children were quartered in the classrooms. There was no privacy barrier. Families were kept intact and food was again provided by the NSV people. So here we lived a day-to-day existence, totally dependent for our livelihood on others, until we were transferred by train to Schwersenz, Poland.

We lived in Schwersenz, much as we did in Litzmannstadt, day-to-day. The only difference worthy of mention was that we lived in big tents with several families per tent. There was no privacy as only sheets separated families. A soft of tedious existence- with people living, dying, birthing, healing, and a hopelessness nurtured by the total lack of control of our own destiny.

We lived day to day, not knowing what the next day would bring or even where we would be. Our evacuations and/or moves were dictated by the war front. Remember we were always at or near the Russian front and our movements were always to escape or stay ahead of the Russians as the German war effort retreated in spurts. And so I don't know how long we stayed in Schwersenz, but in March 1944, we were transported to Puschkau in Poland. This was a resort town, close to Posen (now Poznan). We stayed in Posen long enough to establish a semblance of normal human existence and so I will dedicate a separate chapter to our sojourn in Puschkau.

Puschkau

We arrived in Puschkau in the middle of March 1944 and remained there until January 20, 1945. Here in Puschkau we finally lived in a house again, the first time since we left our own home back in 1943. And although the house was not our own house, life took on a routine if not normal family life. It was wonderful just to be able to call a place "home", even though it wasn't our own. Just living in a house was marvelous. We had several bedrooms, a living room and a kitchen, as well as a balcony, which opened up to a beautiful backyard. There were several other families in the house, as this formerly belonged to a wealthy Polish doctor and his family. Regrettably, the estate and grounds surrounding it were confiscated by the Germans, because the doctor himself had been a member of the Polish underground that resisted the Germans. In retaliation, the Germans abducted and imprisoned the doctor and evicted his wife but let her live in a little cabin on the property, which had until then been occupied by servants of the estate. Mother always felt a little guilty about living in the mansion while the owner was relegated to a servants' cabin. Mother visited the lady often and apologized for the intrusion and invited the lady to visit our portion of the mansion and the beautiful grounds whenever she wanted. However, the lady was afraid of retribution. Mother would always tell her that she would care for our part as though it were our own, so that when the time came for her to reoccupy her home, our portion would be as she left it. This could not be said of other people living in the mansion. In fact, mother was criticized for even talking to the Polish women by some Germans (NSV) who thought that associating or even talking to Poles was below their dignity. But mother, to her everlasting credit, always stood up to such discrimination, telling those who criticized that, had they lost their home and possessions as we had, they would have a greater appreciation for their property and possessions and respect for the property of the Polish people. Mother sure had courage and was willing to risk the animosity of some fellow countrymen (with Nazi affiliation) by doing what she knew to be right. Sure hope some of that courage rubbed off.

Other than that, our stay in Puschkau from March 15, 1944 to January 20, 1945 (about 11 months) was, for the most part, a happy one, for me anyway. Father was offered and accepted a teaching position in a neighboring town (Unterberg) and myself and my sisters enrolled in school. For me it was the beginning of school. I was seven years old by this time- never had a chance to start before. Soon made some friendships and enjoyed what for us had been running for several years- a normal life i.e. school, home, friends, family. The mansion we lived in had a large garden and play-area, a cabin where the poor lady (owner) lived, and to my great delight was backed by a beautiful river (Warthe), just a few hundred yards in the back of the house. The river in fact got me into trouble in an episode I have never forgotten.

Because the river was fast and deep it was off-limits to me, unless accompanied by mother or father or both. At the time of this episode father had been drafted in the army, so mother was left to look after the family by herself. Needless to say, she may have been a bit distraught with the absence of father and the added burden of nurturing the family by herself. Anyway, it was a beautiful spring day and my youngest sister, Lydia, and I decided on our own, to go down and explore the river and its environs. Well, to my great surprise, the ice and snow were breaking up and the ice floe looked ever so inviting for a little ride. When one floated by close enough to the bank I did not hesitate and jumped on for a ride. Well, to my great surprise, instead of landing on the floe, I slipped right through it into the ice-cold water. It was not solid as I had thought, thus it could not support my weight. After all the intervening years- I can still feel the shock of the cold water. Fortunately, the water was not above my head and with the help of my sister, I managed to get out of the water and snow/ice, very wet and very cold. My first thoughts were not of the cold and wet state I was in, but rather how to explain to mother that we had gone to the river without her permission and her presence. Lydia and I came up with the foolish scheme that a neighbor kid, half my age and size had dumped a bucket of water on me. Well- mother didn't buy our story for a second, and before long had elicited the truth. And for the first and only time in my life, I got the whipping of my life from my dear mother. She admitted later in life, that she may have overreacted, but her punishment was not so much for what we had done, but for lying to her. She could not stand lying. I still think it was a culmination of our lying to her and her frustration at father's absence. I think she was a bit overwhelmed by the burden of raising the family single-handedly during such trying times. As for me, it fostered a strong and abiding belief that honesty is the best policy. By the way, Lydia also got a good whipping that she has never forgotten. Ask her sometime.

As stated earlier, I began school in the neighboring town of Unerberg, which was about 2 km from Puschkau. I really disliked school at first, because I didn't know any of the kids, but that soon changed as friendships developed and life between school, family and friends became a normal and ordered routine. I do recall some scary moments (for a seven year old anyway) in that war seemed to be closing in on us again with infernal air raids by the Allies becoming increasingly frequent. It didn't bother me when they occurred at home or at night, because I always felt secure in the presence of family, but the raids were unpredictable and I can recall air-raid sirens while in school. On such occasions school was dismissed, but I still had 2 km to walk home, partway through a forest. These were scary, because as a seven year old I thought they were after me and that I may never see my family again. So I would run and cry all the way home. The Allies, of course, weren't interested in me or our little town, but rather the large, industrial city of Posen. However, the anti-aircraft fire along with bombings and dogfights that ensued frequently were real and very scary events even for adults.

On September 14, 1944, father was drafted into the German army. After basic training in Nuerenberg, dad came home for a brief furlough on January 6, 1945, before being assigned to a reconnaissance unit on the Russian front. After a happy furlough, father's departure was a sad affair needed. Mother and I accompanied father to Posen, from where he joined his troop train destined for the war front. I will always remember vividly the farewell scene at the train station. I was surreal in that on the train ride from Puschkau to Posen I was joking and playing and the thought that he was actually leaving us simply didn't register. But as he kissed us at the station and climbed on the train, then waved through an open window as the train pulled away it hit me. Father was leaving us and we would never see him again. With tears and loud cries I ran after the train, waving to my father and begging him to please come back. Mother, crying herself, chased after me, and had to grab and subdue me. But I refused to be subdued and fought her for a long time not understanding or comprehending that she was helpless and could not keep dad from leaving us behind. I was so struck with grief that I don't recall the trip home from Posen.

Late on the night of January 20, 1945, after we had gone to sleep, there came a knock on the door after 11 pm. When mom opened the door, there was a policeman with a stern order: "this is an order to evacuate immediately! The last train to Germany leaves at midnight. This is your last and only chance to escape capture by the Russian army which is rapidly approaching!" Wow! This left us less than an hour to dress, pack, and get to the train station. Mother made sure we dressed warmly and we took what little we could carry and headed for the train station. At this point, mother recalls leaving behind any and all possessions we had managed to bring from our original home except for important documents and a few photos which mom carried in a pouch inside her dress. That was it!

I would be very remiss if I didn't insert a little side story involving the plight of my oldest sister, Rose. Rose contracted rheumatoid arthritis at an unusually early age and suffered immensely from it. Numerous and different treatments did not offer much help and this insidious affliction not only caused her excruciating pain and suffering but disfigured both her feet and hands. It seemed she spent most of her life bed-ridden. Such an existence would seem untenable during the best of times, yet she survived all the turmoil in our lives. Just the thought of all that suffering pains me even now as I write, many years after her passing. It just doesn't seem fair that one person should bear such suffering. I sure hope and pray fervently that she is being rewarded abundantly by a just and good God. She richly deserves it. In spite of her suffering, I will always remember her great generosity and willingness to help me in any way she could.

And so, back to our evacuation from Puschkau. Rose had just come home from the hospital in Posen. She had rheumatic fever. Somehow, mother with the help of my sisters, Helen and Lydia, got Rose, who was sick in bed, dressed. They put her on a bicycle and the five of us made our way to the train station as fast as we could, fearful that we would miss the train. We got to the train station where a large crowd had already gathered. We left the bike in front of the station and took our place on a train platform awaiting the arrival of the last train. The wait was miserable what with the extreme cold, lack of sleep and lack of space to sit or lie down. Helen decided to ride the bike home to get some blankets even though my mother said "no" (because the train might come anytime). Fortunately, she made it home and came back with the blankets, which we quickly pulled over us. Additionally, the rumble and thunder of the approaching war front added to the chaos and as time went by, the fear that the "last train" to Germany would never arrive.

But arrive it did, about mid-morning the next day. Then there was a mad rush to board the train, with the fear of being left behind driving people to act very aggressively. There was such pushing, jostling, shoving, cursing, crying, and screaming as everyone crowded onto the train.

Sometime around noon the train, loaded beyond its capacity, slowly left the station. Once again, the family was on the move to a destination unknown but nevertheless away from the dreaded Russian front. Before closing the chapter on Puschkau, I should add that in 201, my wife Lucy and I while on a European trip visited Puschkau and specifically the house or mansion we lived in and the train station which was very quiet and serene- the exact opposite of that night of terror experienced 56 years earlier. It left me with some strange feelings or emotions, but also gratitude that somehow we escaped all this and somehow made a good life for ourselves in spite of all the misery. In fact, it is my strong belief that the suffering helped build character and a determination to strive and work hard to improve and never return to such a miserable condition of life.

The train from Puschkau was jam packed with people. At such times all courtesies and manners and human decency vanish and people go into a survival of the fittest mode. A herd instinct takes over and chaos takes over. We traveled on the train for two harrowing days. Late on the first day, mother left the train at a train stop to pick up some water for us, as we were dehydrated and very thirsty. She either got lost or delayed on her way back to the train and was left behind! The next 24 hours were a period of unspeakable fear and horror. Now we were orphans, no mother, no father, and Rose, of course, was sick. For me there was no solace and no sleep as I cried. At this time, Helen took command, to her credit, and became the "head of the household" as she tried to console us and care for us, always leading us in prayer and promising that mother would come back; thus keeping hope alive. Well, the Good Lord must have heard our prayers, for mother had been able to somehow take an express train, that not only caught up to ours but actually passed us and according to some acquaintances who claimed they saw her on the back of her train; waving as she passed our train. To make a long story short, she rejoined us in Spremberg, which was just inside the German border. Finally, our great wish to get to Germany had been realized, but not with the anticipated expectations. Instead of "living happily ever after", we ended up here, only because the town we had been destined for had been destroyed recently and instead of becoming a peaceful heaven for us, the residents of the town themselves became refugees, joining those of us, who had been relegated by events to refugee status.

In reality, we stayed in Spremberg for only one day. Our next stop was Friedrichsheim, where we were picked up by private citizens, who quartered us in their homes.

We stayed in Friedrichsheim for six weeks and we kids went back to school again. As you can imagine, starting up in a new school was never fun. We didn't know anyone and had probably fallen very behind scholastically, as our schooling was always interrupted and short lived or "on the go" so to speak. The wonder of youth is that you are flexible and adjust relatively easily and so even though we stayed in the town for only six weeks, life again began to take on a normal tempo or beat. But the constant rumble of artillery fire, day and night, was a reminder that the war was close at hand and you took it for granted as a way of life. However, air raids, which were carried out day and night, you never got used to. They were just plain scary. They were always preceded by the haunting wail of sirens, followed by beams of searchlights scanning the skies, followed by heavy anti-aircraft fire and the thunder of bombs exploding as they hit their targets. It always seemed like it all happened right above us, and I always found myself wondering in terror "could the next bomb land on us?" In fact, it was always a relief to hear the bombs land elsewhere. We were, I would guess, right at the very edge of the action and it was ferocious. I remember endless military convoys, including machines, guns, and ammunition of every description passing through town heading for the 'front'. We would stand by the roadside looking at the passing soldiers desperately hoping we might glimpse father among them. By this time, communication between father and us had long ceased (via mail). However, at every stop on our journey, mom had always sent dad a card containing our address.

The action around Friedrichsheim was so ferocious that two weeks after our arrival we were alerted to prepare for imminent evacuation as the Russians were closing in. However, a major counter-offensive by the Germans pushed the Russians back and we were able to remain here for six weeks.

On or about March 5, 1945, we were again ordered to evacuate as the 'Russian Front' was collapsing and fighting had reached within 2 km of Friedrichsheim.

We arrived at the train station just after dark. Our train was nothing if not a skeleton of a train. Not a single window was unbroken, seats were broken and filthy and there were no sanitary facilities in working condition. While boarding the train, a huge fire of unknown origin broke out (other than possible sabotage). Just as the fire broke out, the blasted and hated air-raid sirens sounded a warning of imminent attack. Sure enough, within minutes, the dreaded bombing and affiliated anti-aircraft fire broke out all around us. If there had been earlier fearful episodes of our demise, this one topped all the others by far. This was surely it! There was no way we could survive this. The earth was rumbling, people were scrambling and running around in a wild panic, all the while screaming and crying. Miraculously, no bombs hit the station and after due course, the train took off with its cargo of stunned by subdued refugees.

We were on the train for about two days en route to Emmertal, where we arrived on March 7, 1945. By way of explanation; although we spent a lot of time on trains, we didn't cover what would be considered long distances. Travel was always interrupted or delayed at sidings to allow military trains to pass or simply to stop and feed all the people. It seemed there always was chaos and mayhem, and many people committed suicide all along the way, although mother would always try to screen us from these ugly scenes, simply explaining to us that someone had fallen and hurt themselves. It was not until we were older that she told us what really happened.

We arrived in Emmertal late on March 7, 1945. There we were picked up by bus and transported to the small town of Hajen, which is maybe 10 km from the city of Hameln. We were picked up from the bus station by a farmer named Fritz

Holle. We were housed in the second story of his house- we had two rooms. Fritz Holle and his wife lived on the first floor. Both their sons had been conscripted into the German army and thus we took up quarters in what were their rooms. It was in Hajen that the war ended for us. But before it ended let me briefly describe some memorable and poignant moments from my perspective as a seven-year old innocent.

I loved being on a farm. I loved the animals, especially the horses. I would always hang around the barn or stable so I could help cleaning, harnessing, and feeding the horses. Since farmer Fritz had no tractors, all farm work from planting to harvesting was done with the horses. Thus, whenever we went out to the fields we did so on a horse-pulled wagon. One day in the spring of 1945 the farmer and I drove out to the fields to plant some potatoes. This however was not to be one of your run-of-the-mill routines. It in fact turned out to be my first near-death experience. After arriving at the potato field and unloading the seed potatoes and related planting tools, the farmer left to talk to some helpers nearby. I remained on the wagon waiting for farmer Fritz's return. While waiting, a bird or something (I don't know what) spooked the horses and they took off in a mad gallop. I fell backwards in the wagon as it spurted forward, but by grabbing onto sideboards, I was able to right myself, and scramble to the front of the wagon to grab the reins, which were flying loosely in the wind. I managed to gather in the reins and pulled back to stop the horses, but to no avail. The horses were wild and out of control, racing across fields, ditches, and anything that stood in the way. It was so wild that I let go of the reins and held on for dear life. It was, without exaggeration, like the scene from a western movie. I was absolutely terrified! The wind whipped past my face, carrying away with it my tears and screams. Some distance in front of us, there were some neighboring farmers working in the field and they heard and saw the commotion in front of them. They raced on foot to intercept the runaway team, which by now was back on the road galloping at top speed. As we approached our rescuers, who were waving frantically to stop the runaways, the horses swerved in front of them and galloped through a ditch, nearly over-turning the wagon. They continued out to a field that was soft from recent plowing. The fatigue and difficult terrain slowed them considerably and they soon stopped. The rescuers quickly ran over to secure the wagon and horses. I must have been some sight. I was no longer in the wagon, but rather on the tongue or cross-tie (it's the equipment which ties horses to the wagon). Everything also was pretty much gone, including the side and end boards as well as the floorboards. Only the wheels and the undercarriage were left. I don't know how I stayed on that wagon, but at moments such as this your faith in God is reinforced manifold. This could have been a disaster and it about destroyed mother, who as usual blamed herself for allowing me to be on that wagon. Of course, there was no one to blame, including the horses that reacted to an imagined threat. Nevertheless, it left an indelible impression on my mind and even now, I recall my life and family flashing in front of my eyes. I survived and now 57 years later can relate the story.

Life in Hajen prior to the end of the war was quite normal or stable, in the sense that at least we were not on the move. We again went to school and as stated earlier, I loved the farm life and especially the livestock. War was still a reality, but it seemed distant. Slowly the German war effort collapsed. It became very evident as we began seeing more and more deserters sneak through town. These poor soldiers were running and hiding, half-starved, dirty and afraid of being caught. Detection meant a certain firing squad. By the same token, town people were afraid of harboring them, because if caught they would be accused of harboring deserters, which carried heavy penalties. So, these pathetic being slunk around in the shadows avoiding detection and capture.

For mother, life in Hajen, though an improvement was still one of worry and concern. Let me remind you that we were a homeless and penniless family, whose only belongings were the clothes on our backs and a few vital papers documenting births, citizenship, etc. The family lived on food stamps and welfare payments. We hadn't heard from father since he left basic training and therefore did not know whether he was dead or alive. All this weighed very heavily on mother, to the extent that she actually became ill and so weak that she spent much time convalescing in bed. However, no amount of rest could relieve the constant and ever present reality of the hopelessness of the family plight. To help feed the family for example, we kids would go into the forest to pick berries and at other times a seed or kind of nut that could be pressed into oil which in turn could be used for cooking. Certain weeds served for soup. My oldest sister helped farmer Fritz milk the cows and work in the fields for some dairy products as well as vegetables. As for clothes, mother patched clothes until they fell apart. Welfare payments were at less than sustenance level and served primarily to pay for what little food was provided by ration cards. It got so bad that I recall on more than one occasion mother and I would go to neighboring towns and go door to door soliciting (more commonly known as begging) for clothes. Mother always offered to pay for whatever clothes we got by cleaning homes or any other tasks that needed doing. On arriving at home, we would sort through our booty and pick out those items that could be worn (there wasn't much) and the rest would serve for patching other clothes. Nothing was ever thrown out and somehow we managed to scrape through. This was an episode in mom's life that she never would talk about and I'm not sure I should have exposed it. I do so, unashamedly, only to explain our desperate plight during those times.

And so we subsisted until war's end, which happened in May 1945. It just happened one day and began with a rumbling, earthshaking commotion as allied tanks and military equipment approached the town. You could hear them long before you could see them. The fighting was going on in the forest, which was on the other side of the river, Weser, not far from where we lived. There was such panic as townspeople thought we would be attacked and destroyed. The Mayor of the town raised a white flag above city hall as people scurried off to bomb shelters or secure places. We had experienced all this too often and mother very calmly stated that we had nowhere to go and if something indeed happened we would stay together as a family. So we crouched in the corner of the living room and there awaited our fate. My sister Lydia panicked because she feared that this was the end for us. Her hysteria was infectious and shortly I joined her in bawling. Mom very calmly began praying the Rosary, and as it had on so many other occasions, it soothed and consoled Lydia and myself as we awaited our fate.

Suddenly, we could see the Americans or British (I am not sure anymore) Army rolling in the distance. I became mesmerized as I watched mile after mile of military rolling stud come ever closer and closer, then actually enter town, and keep on moving without ever firing one shot. Wow- we looked at each other and smiled, not believing we were still alive. Shortly we went outside and up to the road, where we joined other people as we waved a friendly 'Hello' to our erstwhile enemy. Not one person on arrival was hurt, at least to our knowledge. And when you think about it- what interest would the conquering army have in a little town with no military significance? None, of course. But after all we had been through, and even more for the locals who had really never experienced war or threat of danger, the fear was real. But now it was over and I can still feel the sense of relief. It was over! The family could concentrate on our real problems without fear and without threat to our lives. However, there was still an ever-present concern that required closure. And that was- where was father? More important- was he alive? And if alive, was he still in one piece or was he crippled or disabled? We lived with this ever-present question for several more weeks before it was answered.

And then it happened, on January 18, 1945, while I was playing in the farmyard, minding my own business. Suddenly, I heard Lydia coming into the yard- screaming 'Dad is home, Dad is home'. I looked up, hesitantly, not trusting what I heard. Sure enough there was a smiling man with her and they were headed straight for me. For fear of disappointment, I slowly started towards them, not remembering what Dad looked like and because I did not recognize him. For a second, I thought that he might be an uncle. As I raced up to him, he lifted me and hugged me while repeating several times 'Reinhardlein, Reinhardlein'- an endearing nickname he always called me. With that I knew it was father and at that moment I was without a doubt the happiest kid in the world.

Dad's return was, I believe, a life-saving event for mother. I really believe she would have wasted away if not for his return. In short order she regained her health and strength to become the loving, caring, and vivacious mother we had almost forgotten.

I should also mention my sisters' reaction to father's return. Lydia was the first to see father on his return. She was playing in the street with some other little girls when she saw a stranger approaching them. Father, who recognized her immediately, quietly said 'Lydia' and she in turn, turned to her playmates and whispered unbelievably 'I think that's my father'. Poor thing, she wasn't sure. Father again said 'Lydia, I <u>am</u> your father' (imagine the poignancy). Lydia went berserk and dragged him home, where as I have already described they met me in the yard.

As for Helen, she had gone to the woods to pick some berries or whatever (even certain weeds and mushrooms were used for cooking) when a friend who had learned of Dad's return ran up to her to inform her 'Your father has returned'.

Helen too, like the rest of us, did not immediately believe it. She thought that the friend was joking (sick joke at that) and refused to believe her. Finally egged on by her friend's insistence, Helen ran home to greet and welcome home her father. We laughed and we cried. What an emotional event! One that we will never forget. As for me, this was the happiest day and moment of our lives. The family was whole again. All hunger, poverty, and fear we had experienced could not compare with the vacuum left in our hearts by the absence of father. The family was whole and nothing else mattered. Without exaggeration, the family had been on the brink of disintegration. Consider what might have happened if mother had died (a very real possibility- she was fading and I suspect lost her will to live). Rose was the oldest, but hardly capable of keeping us together because of her own illness. That left Helen, the oldest at about 12 years. She was a take charge and capable girl who behaved like someone much older. Need I say more? So the return of father came at a critical moment in time. Someone greater than all of us must have watched over us. So with Dad's return, the fate of the family takes a huge turn to better and more prosperous times. Yet those years of suffering left deep footprints on all our lives and served as moral anchors or reference points for future behavior and/or character building.

Father, in short order, took stock of our situation and concluded that Hajen did not provide the right environment for raising a family from total poverty and so in October 1945 he moved the family to the town of Holtensen which was on the outskirts of Hameln. He got a job with the British army as a watchman at their base in Hameln. In fact, this was to be an interim job until he could get a position as a teacher. And so we settled in Holtensen in late 1945, in what in former times had been a Gashaus (hotel). Three other families lived in the building, two upstairs (family Katz and family Stollte) and two downstairs (family Diedenhofen and our family). Our quarters included what once must have been a large dance floor with large, beautiful brass fixtures. We used this as our bedroom with three beds. One for Mom and Dad, one for Rose, Helen and Lydia, and one for me. Additionally, we had a fairly large kitchen and our bathroom must have formerly been a lavatory and included three wash sinks and several toilets, none of which were functional. There was a large front yard, which must have served as a Beer Garden during better times. In the yard there was a huge chestnut tree that friends and myself loved to climb. The backyard was huge and one of the tenants (who in later years became Mayor of the town) had served sheds housing a couple of pigs, chickens, a turkey and several geese. I mention the livestock only because they led to significant events in subsequent times. The town itself was small- I doubt it had 1,000 inhabitants, and it was off the main highway and so somewhat quiet and laid back. It was built on a slope which divided the town into what locals called Upper and Lower town. We lived in Upper Holtensen, at the very top of the slope and had a magnificent 360 degrees view of the surrounding country. Holtensen was a pleasant farming community quite affluent at one time. We got to know the farmers quite well in that we all, kids and adults alike, during one season or another, worked on several of them.

We again went back to school, my sisters in Hameln and I began in the local elementary school. They placed me in second grade, which I'm not sure I was prepared for, as until now, my schooling had been sporadic and haphazard at best. Nevertheless, it was a start and I recall having a tough time at first. I had to do homework every day, six days a week. Fortunately, my parents and sisters helped me. Among other things they insisted that I do all my homework right after school. Only after completing my homework was I allowed to go outside and play. I soon developed good study habits early on and in due course was able to hold my own academically and socially. I soon had lots of friends to play with. I loved school and couldn't wait to finish my homework so I could go out to play until dusk. In spring and summer, we played soccer, which is big in Europe, but we also played a version of cops and robbers and war and whatever myriad of games and activities little boys make up and play. One activity I used to love was hiking the countryside as well as the hills and beautiful mountains and forests surrounding it. While in the forest we would pick berries, mushrooms, nuts, and certain edible plants. Remember, there still was tremendous poverty following the war. But, back to the fun times. In spring and summer I also learned to ride my bike. Somewhere, somehow, Dad was able to scrounge up a beat-up old bike that would serve as family transportation and freight hauler. But for me it was a wonderful toy. It was a man's bike and of course I was way too short to straddle the cross bar and so I would be the left pedal in its lowest position, put my right foot and weight on it, then push off with my left foot. This would propel me forward and by repeating this procedure was able to coast down the road. I can assure you there were many spills and even some painful tears until I mastered this process.

One day, while 'riding' my bike, I decided to leave the confines of the immediate neighborhood and go to the top of the hill (maybe 100 or so yards away). Now, the hill represented the end of Upper Holtensen. Down one side led through the town and down to Lower Holtensen. Down the other side was a long (good half-mile estimate) straight right road lined by trees on both sides, which formed a canopy over the road. At the bottom of the hill there was a right hand curve, which continued on into a farming area. There was little, if any, motor traffic. And so I walked the bike over to the hill and did a couple of coasts. I soon discovered that by coasting short runs down the hill, I didn't have to push off with my left foot. In other words, all fun without any work or effort on my part. And soon I made an almost fatal decision. I decided to point the bike downhill and go for a long ride down the road up to the curve. In case you don't envision my impending doom, let me enlighten you.

I started off slowly, and then began gaining speed. This was absolutely exhilarating. I was in seventh heaven. As my speed increased steadily to the point of apprehension, I realized in a moment of panic that I had no way to stop as the bike had only foot brakes and that I could not operate them because I could not reach them mounted as I was. Secondly, I had never needed brakes before. And as my speed increased steadily, so did my predicament. Soon trees were flashing by me and I was approaching the right hand curve at the bottom of the hill. Even with my experience I realized that at the speed I was going, my momentum would make it impossible to make the turn. If that wasn't enough of a dilemma, suddenly I saw a bus approaching the curve from the opposite direction. Oh my! For a split second I thought about throwing myself off the bike, but I couldn't work up the courage. Next thing I remember is that the bus flashed by and I headed across the curve in a straight line and crashed into a hedge that lined the curve. I thought I was dead, another near-death experience, but in addition to numerous scratches, and aches, and pains, I gathered myself together, picked up the bike, slowly limping back home, all the while happy to be alive, yet worried about repercussions from my parents. None came and within days I was back on that bike, puttering, and positioning, bending, and perfecting until I was able to get my right leg under the crossbar and in that grotesque position riding the bike. Chalk the episode up to a respectable up-ticking on life's learning curve. <u>Think before you act.</u>

Life in winter was also wonderful. We used to go sledding every day after school- and after homework. We made runs down the hill (yeah- the same 'bike' hill), under barbed wire and through trees until suppertime and often we would go back out after supper for more of the same. In the evening we used to sled downtown streets especially after a new snowfall. We always rode our sleds on our bellies and used our dangling legs to steer around curves or obstacles. On one occasion, I remember blissfully speeding down a run when a small dog came chasing after me and actually nipped at my leg. While kicking at the dog, I took my eyes off the run. Just then I was rapidly approaching a curve that was lined by a brick wall. When I looked up the wall flashed in front of me. Next thing I remember waking up, with a bunch of people looking over me and a big pain on the left side of my face. Several adults and some friends took me and my sled home, where mother nurtured my wounds, but did not reprimand or scold me in any way. Apparently I had hit the wall head-first and knocked myself out. The left side of my face was split open, but in time a huge scab covered the left cheekbone area of my face and long before it healed I was back enjoying my sled rides, but always with a keen eye open for stray dogs. Another life lesson- be alert!

Life was a hoot! We were materially very poor, but not spiritually. At my age, poverty was a constant. I didn't' know any better, and besides I was having a great time, but I would be remiss if I didn't mention a few of our deprivations: food was at what you would call subsistence levels- i.e. barely enough to survive, but without any frills or excess. In spite of government issued ration cards, we seldom got any meat. To be sure, mother was glad when she was able to get a few bones, since these would at least put a few "eyes" on the soups she cooked. As for milk, only kids under 10 years, I believe, were allowed small rations of skim milk. I have never liked milk in my life, so that never bothered me, but the rest of the family sure would have liked some if only for cooking purposes. And so we supplemented ration cards with what we picked in the forest and also from farmers that we, and even mom, worked for during planting or harvesting. Thus, in spring, children would help in 'thinning' sugar beet plants and in return were fed decent lunches, along with bags of fruit. Mother and other ladies helped harvest sugar beets in fall. In payment they received several sacks of sugar beets, which they would clean and process into molasses, which then could be eaten as a sandwich spread or sent to the factories for processing into syrup and/or sugar. I remember her taking some of that sugar, melting it in a pan and after cooking and hardening, serving it to us kids as candy. Since I had very little, if any, candy during most of our days on the refugee trail, I thought this candy was delicious. In fact, all of us school children used to take lunch to school and since we had little food and certainly no sandwich spread of meat, my sandwich was always jam and bread and mom would sometimes send along a piece or two of the aforementioned homemade candies. One day one of my school mates, son of a local farmer, who always had delicious looking meat sandwiches, asked me what kind of candy I was eating. I told him how good it was and if he wanted I'd be glad to trade a piece for one of his sandwiches. Well, lo and behold, he did like it and we made the trade to my utmost delight. When I told mom about it, she smiled and sent extra 'candy' if available and I kept on trading it for good wholesome sandwiches. The happy state of affairs continued until the boy's mother found out, at which point it abruptly ended. Ah, but it was great as long as it lasted.

Good things occurred, mostly happenstance. As noted earlier, one of the tenants owned some fowl, among which was a turkey. This turkey would scrounge around the backyard and side-yard looking for worms and insects. Well one day, by a stroke of pure luck, mother in looking out the kitchen window saw a large egg in the side yard below our window. What a Godsend. Without any pangs of conscience or guilt she immediately went out and picked up the egg, all the while marveling at the idea of treating the family to a boiled egg which we hadn't experienced in ages. That wonderful turkey supplied us its eggs for a long time. And in a humorous aside, mom tells of a casual conversation with the turkey owner. Said owner described her dismay at the turkey's failure to lay eggs. Since the owner had some chicken and geese that provided plenty of eggs, mom felt morally perfectly justified in her clandestine egg supply.

A final paragraph on that wonderful turkey. One day while pondering how to prepare a family meal with meager foodstuff, the turkey, as if heaven-sent, wandered into the hallway right up to our open door. Without hesitation, my mother threw a few breadcrumbs toward the turkey and thusly coaxed it into the room, whereupon she closed the door and immediately proceeded to kill, and cook the big bird. We ate like kings for the next few days. However, poor mother did some serious soul-searching in justifying her actions. Add to her moral dilemma her fear of being detected. Among other things, the mouth-watering scent that permeated our quarters had to be obscured. That was achieved, primarily as I recall, by keeping the doors and windows locked for several days and not allowing anyone inside. Anyway, everything worked out to our gastronomical delight and there was no remorse. These were tough times requiring tough actions to survive. You did the best you could. Mother did what was necessary to take care of her family. Good for you Mom- I think your actions were justifiable.

Even as a young kid, our dire circumstances apparently evoked some primal instincts that spurred me on to some rather dubious adventures. Having heard mother commiserate often about the lack of food and especially meats, I once took it upon myself to procure some. As stated earlier, one of the tenants in our building had some chickens and as luck would have it, I happened to run across one of the chickens in the backyard. What a meal that would make, I figured. And so without any pangs of guilt or wrongdoing I pounced on that chicken. Now what? How do I kill the bird? Well, how about choking it? And so I struggled with it to grab it by the neck and choke it. After squeezing its neck for some time, I thought the chicken was dead, only to have it start flapping its wings and running away. I re-caught the chicken and repeated this madness two or three times before I lost my nerve and decided it wasn't worth it. That chicken was not going to cooperate and besides it had fought so bravely I decided it deserved to live.

In a lighter vein involving the barnyard fowl, there was my encounter with a gander with a foul temper. I frequently crossed the backyard on my way to school or some other destination. While doing so, I always had to sneak past this mean gander, which had on several occasions taken after me and more than once he came close to catching me. I remember telling my parents about my encounters with that 'goose', which appeared to be as big as me (in my opinion, anyway!). Father laughed and told me 'next time that gander comes after you, just grab it by its neck and squeeze as hard as you can'. Sure enough, shortly after this advice, the gander again charged at me. But instead of taking off in a run for my life, I stood my ground, shaking in my shoes as that huge bird bore down on me. With its wings spread out it was a monstrous size, but when it reached me, I grabbed that bugger with both hands by the neck and squeezed with all my might. And boy was it a struggle. That goose beat the sh__ out of me with its huge wings and it clawed and scratched me with its feet. But I was scared to death and would not release my grip until fatigue from the struggle finally led me to let go, ready to run for my life again. But lo and behold, when I let go, that damn goose took off like a bat out of hell. I was amazed and ecstatic. Never again would that bully challenge me. Blissfully oblivious to my battle scars, I set off to brag to anyone that would listen of my victory over that gander. After that, whenever the bird and I crossed paths, he slunk away. I had obviously gained his respect.

And so life in Holtensen was a fun adventure for me. Oh, we had to scrimp and scrounge but we never starved. All of us kids were doing well in school; there was plenty of time for fun and play. I vividly remember hikes into the hills and forests and on one occasion, a cruise down the Weser River on a Sunday afternoon. Most important, however, the family was whole again and dad was working as a guard at a British military base in Hameln.

One of the benefits of that employment was an annual Christmas party for the children of German employees working there. I'll never forget that party. They served us a wonderful meal. That was followed by entertainment, including my first ever puppet show which I enjoyed immensely. Topping off the evening was the arrival of Santa Claus. As we left the hall that evening every child was given a bag of goodies to eat. Included in the goodies was an orange. I had no idea what it was. I had never seen or eaten one before. I remember mom and dad laughing when I bit into it. They quickly told me that it had to be peeled first. After painstakingly peeling it and before biting into it, I held it up and out for a final admiring inspection. As I held it there in mid-air, I suddenly realized that every eye in the family was glued to that orange, and I suddenly felt a pang of selfishness and an urge or feeling to share it! To a person, they insisted that I eat it myself, saying that sharing it would leave everybody unsatisfied. But I insisted and so they all had a piece and I had the bulk of it. To this day, I feel a warm glow when I think of that moment. I say without hesitation or humility, I did myself proud that day! It was a reflection of how the family survived. We simply shared the good and the bad. In this case it was definitely the good.

And so we lived, or at least I, a very happy life in Holtensen. Many years later, around 1989, while vacationing in Germany with the family, we stopped in Holtensen. After showing the town to Dawn and Lucy (the boys had let us by this time to run the business back home) I recall telling them how much I liked that town and how happy I had been there. And then suddenly it dawned on me, why that town above all others, brought such fond memories. How could I miss it? It was the first place since leaving Neu-Lebental in late 1943 that we had known peace for several years, the family was together and whole, we had made friendships that lasted more than weeks or months, we weren't on the move and there was no fear of tomorrow. And so this place will always remain a kind of renaissance for me- a transition from total turmoil and poverty, to a peaceful, happy, and stable, if not prosperous life. I was a happy kid for the first time in my cognizant childhood.

Furthermore, for the first time in our lives (us children) were able to attend Mass every Sunday. Even though there was no Catholic church in Holtensen, every second Sunday a priest from Hameln was allowed to celebrate Mass in the Protestant church. The other Sundays we walked to Hameln (about 5 km) for Mass. It was always fun. We walked through a beautiful forest, and often other Catholic boys and girls would join us. While we lived in Hajen, Helen received the Sacraments of Penance and First Holy Communion, but Lydia and I received these Sacraments in Holtensen. We used to have Catechism classes every week from Pater (Father) Spang. Also, Fraulein

(Miss) Grete had organized a little group of young people who met often to play games and go for boat rides on the river, Weser. We also took part in some theatre plays, which we performed in various places. These were events we always looked forward to.

And so we lived in wonderful Holtensen until spring 1948. Although Holtensen was a haven for us kids, father had concerns about the family's future. He simply did not see much of a future in post-war Germany. And although the prospect of being assigned a teaching position in the near future seemed to promise better things to come, he felt it would be many years before the reconstruction of the country and the rehabilitation of its social and cultural constitution would be completed. And so when he learned of the existence of relatives in Canada, he contacted them to determine what, if any, opportunities existed in Canada for a fairly destitute family. As a sideline, Father learned of our Canadian relatives from his sisters Helen and Tina, which leads to another sideline. Recall that after leaving Neu-Lebental we had lost contact with both sides of our parent's families. After the war and even during the war, my parents searching through various churches and organizations, including the Red Cross and International Refugee Organizations were able to find some of our relatives. Of the ones they found, almost all were left behind the Iron Curtain. My Aunt Helen who was a widow (her husband had been absconded by the Communists years before), Aunt Tina and husband Nikolai as well as Grandma Siebert, together made it to Germany. We found them living near Hamburg. I recall Father and I making a train trip to their town for a wonderful reunion.

Anyway, getting back to the story, it was then that Dad found out that we had relatives in Canada. As I recall, Father had two uncles and several cousins living in Southern Alberta and an uncle in Ontario. All were farmers. It was they who arranged for us to migrate to Canada. The move was made through the auspices of MCC (Mennonite Central Committee) and sponsorship by our relatives. This meant that we would have to pay the MCC $2,000 (a huge sum for a family that had nothing) and that our relatives would assume responsibility for our well-being; meaning finding housing and work for us. We would find out much later that this was a mistake, for we could have made the move through the auspices of the IRO (International Refugee Organization) at no cost to us whatever and quite possibly moved to the United States instead of Canada. This is not meant to castigate Canada in any way; it means that for Father, the opportunities for employment would have been much better (You'll see later why).

So the decision to emigrate to Canada was made by Father, to the dismay of the rest of the family. Remember that Helen, Lydia and I were happily ensconced in school; Rose in spite of her ever present rheumatism lived and worked at a wonderful convent in Hameln (within walking distance). And Mother especially loved Holtensen and anything German. She would always say "seems like we have strived forever to live in Germany. Finally, we have made it, we are happy, and now we want to leave it. Why?" And Dad would always respond "Look at Germany! Look at us. Neither is going anywhere soon. We have no choice!" And so the decision to leave was made. To the rest of the family, it was, at that moment, a disastrous move. In hindsight, it was the correct decision, but perhaps the most fateful and significant of our lives. For had we stayed in Germany, we can only conjecture what fate awaited us.

In May 1948, we bade a sad farewell to friends. Many asked "Why are you leaving now? Things are and will be getting better all the time. Stay here." And in fact things were getting better (if only because of), Dad being assigned a teaching position in a nearby town. However, the decision to leave was final and so we packed all our meager belongings, and ourselves, into a car (with a driver) supplied by the MCC and moved to a stopover camp called Fallingbostel. Fallingbostel had been a German military base during the war, but now it served as a staging area for emigrants. We lived in barracks that had housed soldiers, two per room. Can you imagine our family of six living in one room? Well, we did for about two months. During that time we were thoroughly tested and checked for diseases and disabilities in preparation for our departure for Canada. The reason for all the testing was to prevent introduction into Canada of any disease or illness. And there to our great dismay, Rose was disqualified because of her health problems and was refused entry into Canada. What a heart-rending moment! How could we leave poor, sickly Rose behind? After much soul-searching and discussion and at Rose's insistence, the decision to leave Rose behind was made. Some serious grieving and shedding of tears followed. Helping us reach this decision was a plan concocted with the aid of the authorities. The plan required that subsequent to arrival and settlement in Canada, and proving financial responsibility; only then, could we bring Rose to join us in Canada. And that, in fact, is what eventually occurred. Rose stayed with some good friends near Fallingbostel for four months before she was allowed to come to Canada.

So, after an unforgettable farewell, we left Rose and by train were transported to Rotterdam, Holland; the point of embarkation to Canada. On July 21, 1948, we boarded the ship *Tabinta,* formerly a freighter, now converted to a passenger ship for our voyage across the Atlantic and to Quebec City in Canada. Our first big meal on the ship was fabulous. We had not enjoyed such a good meal for a long time. Our parents enjoyed a real cup of coffee, which they had not had since the Russian Revolution. Boy, we thought we were in or a real treat. However, the feeling was short-lived; the next morning we were all seasick.

The trip took all of 10 days. We endured and survived an awful storm. At the height of the storm I remember huge waves crashing right over the ship and I found myself wondering why the ship didn't sink. Most passengers, including all our family but me, were really sick. I remember lying in a hammock-everyone lay in hammocks instead of beds, to allow some stability for the rolling of the ship. Now, there were basically two compartments on the ship. All women and children in one, and all men in the other. You can't imagine the stench in our compartment from all the vomiting. As I said, Mom, Helen and Lydia all were sick. I wasn't my usual rambunctious self but I could function. In fact, I felt better out of the swaying hammock and out of the compartment entirely. And so, Mom, worried about Dad's condition, told me to go see how Dad was. To get to the men's compartment you had to cross the mid-section or mid-deck of the ship, and as I came out to cross it, I could see the huge waves washing over the deck. In hindsight, this could have been disastrous for I could have been swept overboard by the huge waves washing over the deck. But in my youthful ignorance, I had no fear and after watching a few moments I decided I could easily make it across the deck if I tried to run between two consecutive waves. And that's what I did. When I opened the door to Dad's compartment I was overcome not only by the stench but the blue cloud of smoke that hung thickly in the room. Can't imagine anyone smoking but they obviously did. And Dad was a non-smoker. When I finally found him, I knew he was a very sick man. He looked awful and his barf bag was full. He told me he was okay and he did survive, of course, but I did not linger any longer than necessary and got the heck out of there and back to report to Mom that although sick like most others, he was alive.

Like I said, other than the storm and the delay it caused in our passage, the sail to Canada was quite uneventful. We arrived in Canada at the port of Quebec City, province of Quebec on August 1, 1948. Except for Helen, none of us could speak any English. All around us in the terminal people spoke in a tongue we did not understand and all message boards and signs were meaningless. To her credit, Helen already had two years of French and three years of English, and so could ask some simple questions. She was our go-between in our new country. Mother was pretty disillusioned- and she would say "Before we were in Germany where we didn't have anything, but at least we could talk with people and read the language. Now we still have nothing and we can't even communicate with anyone. This will be the end of us." Poor mom- it was tougher for her than any of us, although I suspect Dad had some second thoughts. After the perfunctory passport checks we were taken from the port to the train station where we boarded a train for the long trip across Canada to the prairie province of Alberta. Traveling through the provinces of Quebec and Ontario was quite interesting from a scenic viewpoint- many lakes, rivers, creeks, and miles and miles of forest. When we approached Manitoba, the topography changed from green, lush landscapes to dry, barren, and ever so flat and boring prairie land. It was quite monotonous. Arriving in Winnipeg, the capitol of Manitoba, the train stopped for several hours and we were able to walk a short distance to the center of the city. I was amazed at the large number of cars in the city. I recall standing on an overpass and just watching the auto traffic in utter amazement at the traffic maze. Continuing on from Winnipeg, we traveled for several more days across the boring desert until we arrived in Bassano, Alberta, our final rail destination. Bassano was a two-horse farming town. We were the only passengers that got off there. As we stepped out onto the wooden platform and looked around, we were struck by the endless nothingness, as we slowly made the 360 degree turn to survey our future homeland. Father's cousins, the Peters' family, were at the station to greet and welcome us. After a proper greeting, we and our meager belongings were packed into Cousin Henry Peters' car and carted off to their farm in Gem about a 20 mile drive across dirt roads.

The Peters' operated a small farm located less than a mile from Gem. If Bassano was a two-horse town, then Gem was a one-horse town consisting of a General Store that also served as a post office, service station, and a lumber yard. That was it! The biggest down (Bassano) was at least 20 miles distance. For us this was as mother always put it- a wilderness. Gophers and coyotes far outnumbered people. The only human contact was made by going to the general store and/or going to Mennonite church services on Sunday. I didn't much care for the long services, but I did enjoy the good food that always followed the service.

Now, our stay on the Peters' farm was only temporary, serving as a stay over until Dad found a job and living quarters for the family. Thus, we stayed on the farm about one week or so. Somehow our family of five and Peter's family of seven were able to squeeze into their small farmhouse- there were people in the living room and kitchen. We helped on the farm in every way we could, from milking to tending the animals, gardens, and fields. The Peters' had a son, Ernie, who was my age and we immediately connected. We were together from morning to night; in fact we slept in the same bed. Ernie was a fun kid who taught me how to use a softball glove, how to drive a tractor, and even tried to teach me some English. He spoke a broken German, but we had no problem communicating. And so our stay on the Peters' farm, although very cramped and difficult for the adults, was a fun time for me.

As I said earlier, our stay with the Peters' served as a stopover until father could find something permanent in the way of employment that would provide both work for Dad and shelter for the family. Well, it turns out; Dad had an uncle- Aaron Koop- in Spring Coulee, Alberta, where he operated a big farm by their standards. Now my grandmother, (Dad's mother- Helen Koop) who had arrived much earlier and by another route, with Aunt Helen, was living with the Aaron Koop family. Aunt Helen had found a job as a housemaid in Pincher Creek. Uncle Aaron was quite advanced in age and only one of his half dozen children remained home to help run the farm. Thus he needed a farm hand to help out and knowing of our arrival from Germany, he and his wife and Grandmother came to visit us at the Peters' home. After a proper welcome and a big meal and much gossip, he told Dad of his need for a farmhand and offered Dad the job if he wanted. Included in the job offer was full lodging and board for the family in their home. After due deliberation and urging by Grandmother who wanted us to join her, Dad accepted the offer and preparations began for our move to Spring Coulee, which was probably 150 to 200 miles from Gem. Our farewell from the Peters' was hard for me, as I had enjoyed living on the farm and of course had grown very fond of my cousin Ernie.

And so we traveled to Uncle Aaron's farm in Spring Coulee, to live with the Koops and Grandmother as one big, happy family. As I recall it, that farm was a wheat farm out in nowhere. There was nothing but rolling hills of wheat fields or hay fields. I don't remember how far the nearest farm was from us, but you could not see any neighboring farm and I am not sure whether this was due to distance or invisible because of the rolling hills. Either way, we felt very isolated. "The end of the world" as Mother lamented.

And life with the Koops was no picnic. Uncle Aaron's wife Helen was very fussy about her home. Everything was spic and span. Now enter a family of five, including a rambunctious ten-year-old boy, to join four adults and her sedate lifestyle was shaken to the core. Time and again I was admonished for messing things up, making too much noise, slamming the doors, failing to take off shoes, abusing furniture, etc. etc. I was not a happy camper! Neither were Mother, Father, sisters, and Grandmother too. Mom always felt guilty for things I did and never felt at home, even though she did the bulk of the housework, with help from my sisters. Dad was worked like a slave, from daybreak to sunset and beyond. We happened to arrive during haying time. In those years, or at least on this farm, everything was done manually. The hay was loaded by hand onto horse drawn hay wagons. When the wagon was full it was taken to a barn or haystack where it was unloaded again by hand and neatly stacked. This was hard work performed in extremely hot weather. Dad's arms and legs swelled up and were so painful in the mornings especially, that he could hardly move and it pained Mother, and all of us to see him like that. Our "good" Uncle Aaron joked about it, calling Dad a "wimp". He of course did very little but supervise, while his son did the easy chores such as driving the horses or the device that conveyed the hay to the top of the stack or barn where Dad had to pick it up and stack it neatly.

As for me, I was bored to tears. There was nothing to do and nobody to do it with. I was promised a pony, which never happened and my only companion was a dog. Seems like the only exciting thing I could do was getting into trouble. For example, I once got inside the farm truck, which was parked on a slope. After playing with all the gadgets in the truck, I managed somehow to shift it out of parking gear and it rolled backward, eventually coming to rest, after knocking down a picket fence. I felt pretty bad, but they never let me forget it.

And so life continued with new strains and stresses developing as time when on. Adding to the strain, for me anyway, was a ritual the Koops developed of having my sisters sing for visitors and myself reciting poems. Thus, on Sundays when folks came to visit, Helen and Lydia had to sing and then I had to recite a poem in German. Sometimes the visitor would give me a coin as a reward and made a big deal out of it. I disdained the coins because I had no place to spend them- I didn't eve know the value of the coins. Not only did we perform on the farm, but we had to go to nondescript Mennonite churches way out in nowhere and after the service, we had to perform to the accolades of the few that were present.

An interesting event occurred when Uncle Aaron took all of us to a Hutterite farm on a Sunday. Now the Hutterites are a religious sect very similar to the Amish in our own country. They operate hugely successful collective or community farms with everybody chipping in. The families live in their own dwelling but eat together and work together. They are mostly self-sufficient by growing their own foods, sewing their own clothes (all black) and building their own homes. Their only concessions to the secular world were farm mechanizations.

They use state of the art farm equipment, unlike our Amish who still manage with horses. They are excellent farmers and by most standards of substance quite affluent, but they don't' flaunt it, but rather plow their earnings back into their farm. When we arrived there, they greeted us quite warmly, speaking in a dialect of German that we could understand. They knew Uncle Aaron from previous visits. After showing us the farm, livestock, implements, school, church, etc. they invited us to eat dinner (lunch) with them. They served all their meals in a huge mess hall. The food was very good. The kids, in fact all the people, were friendly though somewhat shy. For me, all this was quite interesting; if not appealing considering that we had experienced communal living at its worst during our trek through the war. On leaving, the Hutterites sent along much food and drink, which I later learned, was the true reason for Uncle Aaron taking us there. He used us as a pretext for a visit, knowing it would end with a generous gift of food. Knowing this, my parents refused future invitations for "Hutterite visits" from Uncle Aaron. He abused their generosity.

We suffered our stay in Spring Coulee one month, but mom and dad soon realized we were in a dead end predicament. We realized our "good" relatives were using us. As mom put it "they would have worked dad to death". There wasn't going to be a house for us, and we would have to all live together in that infernal house with Aunt Helen lording it over all of us. Mom was afraid the kids would grow up wild. Add to this, our disdain for attending Mennonite church services. We were Catholic and mom especially was a "solid Catholic". It wasn't just attending Mennonite services, but doing it under the fake pretense of being a Mennonite and calling ourselves Mennonites. This was so, because on emigrating under the auspices of MCC (Mennonite organization for refugees), we were told we had to be members of the Mennonite church, so we agreed to be "Mennonite" in name. So now here we were (Mennonites in name only) in the midst of relatives who all were Mennonites (Dad was a Catholic convert) who insisted on taking us to their church and introducing us as Mennonites. Though they knew the truth, they felt because of their sponsorship we owed it to them to join their faith. Thanks to mother's strong resistance we remained true to our faith even though others thought otherwise. In a nutshell, Mom and Dad decided we had to leave Spring Coulee for the sake of the family and after some serious discussions with Uncle Aaron, who was deeply disappointed, the search for a new start commenced.

Eventually, Father found a job as a farm hand with a farmer, John Neufeld, in a place called New Gem. If Spring Coulee was a desolate place, then New Gem had to be a mere speck of dust, out in nowhere. There was no store, no church, and no business of any kind. Only a one-room school was all that served as a community center worthy of a name. The school will be described later.

The Neufeld's farm was a combination of farm and ranch in that John grew some grain crops as well as alfalfa. These served mainly as fodder for his cattle, which had to be fed in the winter months. But the bulk of the land was just plain rangeland for his huge herd of cattle. These cattle were wild and remained on the range all year except the winter months when they were fed. Some domestic cows, pigs, chickens, sheep, etc. were kept to feed the family.

These cattle were wild, and remained on the range to forage all year long. Only in winter, when foraging was slim and difficult, loads of hay were spread out on the prairie regularly to feed them. The only time you would see much of them was when they were brought in for marketing, or for branding, dehorning, or for castration of the male calves. A large corral served this purpose. But more about the cattle and ranching later.

As stated earlier, Dad was hired as a ranch hand at $100 per month. This was 1948, and though the price index was only a fraction of what it is today, $100 per month for a family of five is hard to imagine. To make things worse, we owned the MCC (Mennonite organization that sponsored our trip from Germany to Canada) $2,000, a huge sum at that time. A somewhat dismal beginning to our new life. Add to this our new home, which I shall now describe. To call it a house would be a gross exaggeration. It was in fact a ramshackle chicken coop that had been converted into a two-room shack. The rooms were no more than 10 feet by 10 feet each. One served as kitchen, dining, living, and family room. The other held two beds (one was a cot, the other a double bed) and a smaller dresser. My grandmother, who had left Uncle Aaron with us, slept on the cot. Mother, Father, and I slept in the double bed. Helen and Lydia had to take their bedding every night to the farmer's house to sleep in their kitchen. In the morning they had to roll up their bedding and return to our shack. In the kitchen we had a coal and wood-burning stove that served as both a stove and furnace. Our kitchen table was a wooden crate about 3' x 2' x 2' that had been used to carry our belongings from Germany. Wooden apple crates served as chairs. The only other piece of furniture in the kitchen was an old cupboard which housed all the dishes and pots and pans. There was no indoor plumbing or electricity. An outhouse served as toilet and a beat up old basin happened only once a week and the same water served the whole family, one at a time of course (and as I recall it, I was always the last because I hated baths). Water was retrieved by bucket from a cistern. Bathing water was heated in a large tank built into the stove and it took a long time to heat. That explains why bathing was such a big event that occurred only once a week. Obviously there was no sewage system and all water was simply thrown out behind the shack.

Winters in Canada are extremely old. I recall a 1" to 2" coat of ice covered the walls in our bedroom, which was unhcated. We always wore full-length underwear and socks to bed. At night, prior to going to bed, Mom or Dad would place large, slow-burning chunks of coal in the stove, to provide some heat until dawn.

For lighting the shack we used a kerosene lamp, an extremely dangerous fire hazard in such tight quarters. In the morning, mom would light the lamp then stoke whatever embers remained in the stove, add coal from the coal bucket, and fire it up. Then she would break up the ice that covered the surface of the water in the water bucket prior to making breakfast. By the time I would get up, the kitchen was always warm and food was on the table.

In addition to a $100 salary, the Neufelds gave us a cow, a pig, and several chickens, as well as access to the garden. This was very generous as the animals provided us with all our dairy, meat, and egg products. The garden provided us with potatoes and vegetables throughout the year. Those vegetables, which could not be kept fresh, were canned in glass (Mason) jars. Thus, with housing and food covered, the only goods that had to be purchased were clothes. And here mom helped enormously for not only did she sew and knit many of our clothes, but they lasted forever as she would mend any tears or damage. We never had boots in the winter and to keep our feet warm we would wrap them in rags before putting on our shoes. And so not only were we able to survive on $100 a month, but were able to put away small sums to pay for a $2,000 debt.

The Neufelds were good to us and although the work was hard, everybody pitched in to do their share. Although our humble abode was not worthy of being called a house, we did not have to share it with others and so we were content. The Neufelds had three children. The oldest, Henry, was about

Helen's age (about 15) and had a severe stutter. The second oldest was a girl named Wilma. She was about my age. And the youngest was a boy, Rudy, of five or six years.

About a half mile from the Neufeld homestead was the farm of Henry Neufeld who was John's brother. They had two boys, one about Helen's age and one about Lydia's age. The two farms, being adjacent to each other, with two brothers as owners, meant that a lot of the farm and ranch work was conducted with everybody chipping in to do common farm chores. Thus at round-up there were six men to handle the range herds. All of course were good horsemen and their horses were trained to handle all those wild doggies. I too soon learned to ride quite proficiently and loved every ride I ever took except one, which I will discuss later.

For me, life on the farm was an adventure. In addition to riding the horses, I remember times when, together with the older boys, we would ride calves and even steers. Needless to say, there was much good-natured teasing and laughing as one after another were bucked off whatever we were riding. These darn critters just couldn't' stand having someone on their back. But we got pretty good at it. I also enjoyed watching the adults as they performed chores such as branding calves, dehorning the cows so they couldn't hurt each other, and castration of male calves. They were very good at doing these jobs and well they had to be because there was so much bawling and distress during branding and/or castration. At first it bothered me, because it seemed very cruel, but I soon got over it, being told by the adults how it was all for the good of the calves. But the sounds of calves bawling and the smell of blood and burning flesh are still quite fresh in my mind.

Winter came quite early and soon we were covered with a thick blanket of snow. Lakes and swamps froze over solid and it was time for trapping. There were many weasels, muskrats, badgers, coyotes, and even wolves on the prairie and in winter folks would go trapping for fur. I would go along with the Neufeld boys to set the traps at various locations on the frozen-over swamps, but usually where there were telltale signs of activity, such as little mounds or entrances to underground boroughs and dens. We put some bait in the traps, set them, and anchored them so the captured critters could not run away with the trap. A week later we would return to retrieve our booty. As I said before I used to enjoy all this until one day we came to a trap at a muskrat den. What I saw changed my mind about trapping forevermore. There in the closed trap was all that was left was a leg. The leg's owner, in its desire to free itself, had chewed off its own leg. That bothered me to this day and I never again went trapping. In retrospect, it may seem cruel by today's standards of treating animals, but within the context of life on the farm in those times our methods were neither callous nor unusual but in fact were normal and acceptable. Nowadays that would no longer hold true, but it illustrates our civil evolution since then.

Earlier I mentioned how much I enjoyed the farm/ranch life and especially horseback riding. We would ride both bareback and with saddle depending on our sense of urgency. However, there was one wild ride that will forever stand out above all else. One day while walking home from school, one of the Neufeld boys who had ridden to school, for some reason was unable to ride home. He asked me if I would ride it back to the farm from where his brother would then give me a double-ride back to my home. I couldn't hide my excitement as I eagerly accepted the offer. Now I was a pretty decent rider, but this horse was a small, somewhat wild Indian pony that could only be ridden bareback. No problem! I immediately mounted the little pinto and began to ride home. Everything went as expected, then for some inexplicable reason, the horse bolted and took off helter skelter, in the process depositing me on the ground. After regaining my balance I latched onto the horse's mane with one hand and with the other tried to reign in the panic-stricken horse. Something, and to this day I don't know what (maybe it was our shadow), had spooked the pony and it took off like a cannon. The wild whistled past my ears and the horse's mane whipped my face. And so, in sheer terror with tears streaming over my cheeks we raced towards home. But despite my terror, couldn't help notice how smooth the rise was, almost like sailing through the air. It seemed the horse's hooves hardly touched the ground.

When my horse took off, the other Neufeld boy took after us in order to catch up and stop my horse. Although his was a bigger horse, he never did catch us. All I remember is him shouting something about "Hang on. I'll catch you." Fear is a greater incentive for speed than size, and so my smaller horse with its "imagined" fear could not be caught. We flew along until we approached the entrance to the horse's farm and for a brief moment it tried to make the turn. Had it made that turn, there was no way I could have stayed on its back and would have continued in a straight line until deposited on the ground. Fortunately, the dumb thing realized couldn't make the turn and so continued on the road. Strangely, after passing the farm entrance it slowed considerably either because fatigue set in or it calmed down, or both. I too calmed somewhat, but for some reason convinced myself that the horse would go on forever, that I would somehow end up way out in the wilderness, never to see my family again. Silly now, but not then, at that age. Anyway, I decided that my only escape would be to throw myself off the horse. I hesitated at first, but finally built up the courage to dive off the horse. I landed head first, with the brunt of the force on my left shoulder. My head was fine, but boy did my shoulder hurt. Nevertheless, I was relieved to be on terra-firme. To my great surprise, as soon as I threw myself off, the horse immediately stopped a few feet from me and stayed there. It was only after I collected myself and my thoughts, that I remembered this was a cow-pony. All I had to do was to make a move as if to get off and the pony would stop immediately as it had been trained, i.e. when a cowboy ropes a calf or steer, and while he dismounts, the horse stops to help the rope hand.

Of course in my panic, all reason left and I ended up eating dirt. Shortly, the other rider caught up and helped me onto his horse, as I was not about to get on the pinto and we proceeded towards home. My shoulder was hurting and I didn't dare move it. A stab of pain passed through my shoulder at every step of the horse. I thought the trip home would never end. I was in agony when we got home. Mother made me as comfortable as she could. By now there was a knot on my left collarbone and swelling around it. Mom thought it was broken and that I should go see a doctor. But the nearest doctor was miles and miles away and so mom immobilized my arm (and subsequently the shoulder) and put me to bed. Over the next month or two I was unable to use my left side because of the pain, but eventually it healed. So much for the medicine in those times. The only cure to an ill or affliction was, let nature take its course. It did, and we survived.

And now, let me describe school. The school was a one-room school, with a pot-belly stove in the back to keep us warm in the winter. A coal bin in the porch of the school held the coal that fueled the stove, which I recall at times became red hot. There was one teacher serving nine students. The students (pupils) were enrolled through the grades as follows: one in grade nine, three in grade eight, two in grade six, one in grade five, one in grade four, and one in grade one. Sister Helen was in grade eight and sister Lydia in grade six. Both had studied some English back in Germany. As for me, having no training in English, I was put in grade one. Boy was that a demotion. I should have been in grade four. I sure didn't like going back to grade one. And so I started with the "Dick and Jane" reader. As for arithmetic, I've forgotten where I fit in except that when the teacher worked with the kid in fourth grade I followed the math exercises privately, easily understanding and doing them because math of course is international and languages is not a barrier. To make a long story short, I did all my Dick and Jane reading and writing in quick order, then would get bored and listen in on lessons addressed to the other grades. Remember we were all in the same room.

I always enjoyed and couldn't wait for recess. It was here we played the usual kids games, but I learned to play softball, including use of the baseball glove. We also played "anti-one-over". (Two teams were on each side of the school and we would throw the ball over the roof and run to the other side of the school to catch somebody to make him out.) It was lots of fun. The teacher was Arthur Loewen (a Mennonite). All the kids got along well with each other and in retrospect I consider my experience in a one-room school, well- interesting. Frankly, under the circumstances, I don't think it stunted my educational development. The only element that may have stunted my assimilation into the Canadian culture was the fact that all the school kids were Mennonite and as such they spoke a little German, and consequently we communicated in German. My learning English may have been slightly delayed by the circumstances. However, let me add that in spite of this slight handicap, I was completely fluent in English before the school year ended. And to those who would say that you need a bilingual approach for non-English speaking kids, I say HOGWASH. Total immersion in English is not only the best, but the only way. I speak of personal experience and the experience of many other kids in my shoes.

While speaking of school, I should mention there was no school bus. We walked about one mile to and from school every day, even through rain and snow. In fall, after school began this was no problem, as it was warm, but after the first snow it became increasingly (difficult) due to the cold and the depth of snow that we had to trudge through. We had no overshoes or boots, but walked in our shoes, our feet being wrapped in warm rags to guard against the cold. Many days we'd spend several minutes around that wonderful pot-belly stove thawing out. At night we'd do the same after arriving at home. At times the wind would be howling causing the snow to drift to the point that you could hardly see where you were going. But the snow wasn't all bad. I remember with joy the sleigh rides, snowball fights, building of snowmen and just fooling around in the snow until we were either soaked or cold to the bone. And how good it felt when you went inside and the drowsiness and sound sleep that followed after a hearty meal.

And so, life was good. I had no worries. My only concern was having a good time. But not quite so for my parents! They were naturally concerned about the family's future. We were far from owning a home of our own. Dad's job was tenuous, in that the crops were in, with the farm workload way down for the winter. And mom and dad had that cursed $2,000 debt to MCC. As work on the farm slowed down, Dad would get the odd job at neighboring farms, building barns, or rebuilding buildings. In the meantime, the six of us suffered in our tight quarters. Sometime towards the beginning of winter of 1948, a neighboring rancher, for forgotten reasons, moved out of his homestead thereby leaving a spacious home empty. I don't remember the details or circumstances by which it came about, but to our great relief and delight, we were allowed to move into their home rent-free. To us this was so spacious, we thought it a palace. No more did Helen and Lydia have to go to the Neufelds to sleep. And for me, no more sleeping together with Mom and Dad in the same bed and with Grandma in the same room. Dad would still work for the Neufelds off and on and we were a little closer to school. And so we settled into our new palace. Talk about room. There was enough for all of us and we could probably have housed a few more people. Only problem was heating this monster. It was like living in a refrigerator, but we were always grateful for our good fortune. Not only did we have a huge house, but there were good warm barns to shelter our animals and there was enough hay and fodder to feed them until summer or the next harvest. What little else we needed we could get from the Neufelds.

While living in our new "palace" there were several significant events that occurred and are worthy of mention. First and foremost, word arrived from our dear sister Rose that she had been cleared for emigration to Canada. You can't imagine the joy that filled our home. We couldn't wait for her arrival and didn't want to completely believe until she arrived in person. But arrive she did and there is nothing to say, but our happiness was complete! Our family was complete! It doesn't get better than that. Rose soon found a job as a housemaid on a farm in Old Gem, and though she had some tough times, because she didn't speak English, the important thing was she was home (even if not in our house).

The other event worthy of note has darker connotation or implication, but is important to point out the fragility of our existence. Anyway, one day sometime in the middle of winter, a large herd of cattle either by hunger or pure chance wandered into the farmyard. Now, the timing was by design, or so it seemed to mom and dad, for we had run very low on meat and being heavily dependent on meat for our diet, the question was how do we replenish our meat stock. On seeing the large herd milling about the yard, and not knowing who they belonged to, my parents decided that they would pick out an unbranded steer and butcher it. To hear Mom tell the story, they were scared to death, not only by the thought of being detected, but the guilt they felt at committing this act. But again, survival and welfare of the family overrode feelings of guilt. And so, they waited until sunset (up there in the winter the sun set around 4:30 pm) and then with a bucket of grain my father goaded a young steer into one of the barns. Once inside, Mother closed the door, and while the steer was feeding out of the bucket which Dad had placed on the ground, Dad picked up a large axe and with the blunt end struck the steer in the front of his head. The steer was stunned and fell to the floor. Dad placed another blow to the same sot, and then slit the steer's throat. Fortunately, there was a lot of straw in the barn to absorb the gushing flow of blood. Dad later told us how he worked late into the night digging a hole in the frozen ground in which to dump all the blooded straw and to hide the innards of the steer. He also told of scrubbing the floor of the barn to remove any trace of blood. Needless to say, both

Mom and Dad worked all night cutting up that steer and hiding any trace of its existence.

The episode was like a nightmare for my parents and I never knew about it until years later when mom told me. I do, however, remember that at one point while living in that "palace" we enjoyed an unexplained abundance of good meals.

One final episode will end our sojourn in New Gem." While still living in the "palace" there was a rather humorous incident involving mother. It so happened that a neighboring rancher by the name of Mr. Peak, along with a number of cowboys, were rounding up a large herd of range cattle from nowhere to somewhere, for whatever reason I don't know. Now, we had a little piggy given to us by Mr. Neufeld, which used to freely roam around the yard. While the herd of cattle moved past the yard, that silly little pig joined the herd and wandered with it. Mother saw this and panicked, thinking the little pig would get trampled. So she ran after the herd, arms waving desperately trying to get the attention of Mr. Peak. When he finally saw and acknowledged her she excitedly said "Mr. Pig" and waving at the little pig shouted "Peak, Peak". She didn't know but a few (English) words including "pig", but in her excitement she called him "Mr. Pig" and the piggy she called "peak" which was the man's name. The man to his credit was not disturbed by being called a pig, but he didn't know what she wanted. Lydia and Helen ran after the little pig to catch it; but the faster they ran, the faster the cattle ran and the little pig with them. Finally, the pig was caught, but Lydia and Helen had nothing to hold it. Helen saw a piece of barbwire, picked it up, and put it around the pig's neck. They were just starting on their way home when Mr. Peak saw them. He drove his truck to where they were and loaded the pig and them on the truck and drove them home. Later that night at supper the family enjoyed a good laugh when mother recounted her experience with "Mr. Peak". She didn't think it all that funny and felt bad about calling the good man Mr. PIG. "It's okay Mom" we told her. We had many laughs about this incident.

And so life continued during our stay at the "palace". The walk to school was shorter and thus less demanding. School itself went well, although doing grade one level was extremely frustrating for me, but I picked up the language. As stated earlier, all the other kids spoke a broken or dialect German and this probably slowed the process of learning English. In my opinion, immersion is the only path to language proficiency and subsequent assimilation.

Some school highlights worthy of mention were the preparation for Halloween, Christmas, and Valentine's. These were all big events, especially Halloween and Valentine's, as those were something new for my sisters and me. I recall drawing or painting cards and placing them all over the windows. Then at Halloween and Valentine's, we would have a special lunch and/or dinner, including absolutely delicious homemade ice cream. At Christmas, all the families joined in an evening of celebration. All we students actually put on a Christmas play that we had worked on and rehearsed for weeks prior to Christmas. All the adults were properly impressed if measured by their enthusiastic applause and kudos. We kids, of course, were tickled pink. The play was followed by good food, an exchange of gifts and community caroling. All this with the pot-bellied stove glowing red as it kept us warm and cozy, while outside it was cold and snowing. What a beautiful scene out there in nowhere. I still get a warm glow as I revisit that wonderful scene.

` All went home that night content and at peace, counting their blessings. In our family there were mixed feelings. We had a lot to be thankful and grateful for. First and foremost, our family was together, nothing could be better than that. And there was no more hunger, no fear of war, or the informal evacuations that had been our lot during the war. And so, in retrospect, though dirt poor, we were safe and content with our lives. My parents' concerns for the future were of no concern to me and my biggest concern was figuring out how and where to have fun. As mentioned earlier, apart from school, hunting, trapping, riding horses and calves, and flying kites in spring took care of time spent outside of school. One incident that wasn't necessarily noble or even upright occurred when one farmer and his wife left for vacation. In those days, life was simpler- people were much (more) trustworthy, and crime in such a rural environment was non-existent. And so true to this ethic when this farmer couple left for a few days, they left everything including the house unlocked. Well, several of us boys, while on our way to our traps, took a shortcut through the absent farmer's yard, knowing full well that they were gone. Being boys, we also were in search of a "smoke", knowing also that this farmer was a smoker. And so we just went into the unlocked farmhouse, found the can of tobacco and also the papers and proceeded to make a "roll-your-own", which the older boys then jointly smoked. We knew what we did was wrong, but we also thought it was exciting. Anyway, we never did take anything else and except for the "roll-your-own" cigarette, left everything untouched. Imagine if you will, leaving a home unlocked nowadays. What we did was mischievous, but at no time was there any intent or wishes to commit a crime. Yes, life was simple, as were the people, and so in many respects the quality of life then was superior to today's crime-ridden rat race.

I failed to mention earlier that Dad's employ at the Neufeld farm was in part due to an illness that limited Mr.

Neufeld's ability to work. As fall and winter passed that affliction gradually improved to the point where together with his son(s), Mr. Neufeld would no longer need Dad's help. Thus, we were once again forced to look for a home and employment elsewhere. It so happened that we had relatives in Coaldale with a farm. Among the crops cultivated were sugar beets. These required manual thinning and hoeing in spring and summer and manual harvesting in fall. This back-breaking work was usually done by temporary workers or immigrant families such as ours. And so in April of 1949, we moved from New Gem to Coaldale, to work on cousin George Kopp's farm. George Kopp was Dad's cousin and he had a family of four or five young kids. In addition to his immediate family, cousin George's father, my grandmother's brother, lived on the farm in a separate, small home.

As for us, we were relegated to a three-room shack that was a half-mile removed from the Kopp farmstead. There was no porch; in fact, there wasn't even a stairway to the front entrance. Several bricks served as stairs. As to the approach from the road, it went through a deep ditch, which after a rain was non-transversal, until Dad built a simple footbridge. The house had neither paint nor insulation and consisted of a tiny bedroom, decent size kitchen and combination living room/ bedroom. My sisters and I slept in the small bedroom with Helen and Lydia in the larger of the two beds and I in the smaller cot. Dad, mom, grandmother and Rose (whenever she came home) slept in the farthest reaches of the living/bedroom. The kitchen served as kitchen, dining room and family or all-purpose room. There was a stove in the kitchen which was used for cooking and heating in cold weather. An additional pot-bellied stove sat in the middle of the living/bedroom, but was seldom used, in order to save coal and because the room was used sparingly during the daytime. The outside walls had cracks or slits in them that you could look through.

As for our yard, Dad built a makeshift barn out of scrap lumber, and it housed our cow, several pigs, chickens, and ducks, which we had brought from New Gem. Next to the house and barn was a pond which provided water not only for us. This was standing water that was used by animals, birds to drink, swim, and muck around in. In the summer, a thick scum covered it. It was not fit for human consumption. We used water mostly from the irrigation ditch near our house. Mom would boil all the water needed for drinking or cooking, but not that water which was used for washing clothes or bathing. She must have done a good job as none of us ever got seriously ill. We also used rainwater and melted snow for drinking and cooking.

And so we settled into this place. It was April and farm work was a couple of months off, giving Mom and Dad time to fix up the place as best they could. As for my sisters and me, we immediately had to register at school. We lived about three and a half miles from school and were bused in daily, Monday through Friday. This sure beat walking as we had done in New Gem.

The first ride to school was memorable. The ride itself was enjoyable, with a load of thirty plus kids. It was noisy, but exciting. I was duly impressed when we entered the town of

Coaldale which seemed like a large city to me, (only 1,500 people) considering we had spent the previous eight or nine months in places such as New Gem which had nothing. And when we got to school I was overwhelmed with all the kids (probably more than 300 total) and such a big school. We were lost and, but for the help of the bus driver, had no idea where to go or what to do. It was very intimidating. Well, the good man took us straight to the principal's office. The principal, Mr. Baker was an elderly and very kind man who gave us a warm welcome. After some perfunctory comments and checking of our report cards from New Gem, he filled out our registration forms and assigned us to our classrooms. In my own case, however, he was a little baffled, asking me "what grade were you in?" I told him that I was in grade one, but should really be in the fourth grade. He said, "Well, there are only three months left in the school year and you missed the first seven months. Do you think you can catch up with the class?" To which I replied, "even though I was in first grade at New Gem, there had been a fourth grade student in New Gem and I would always listen in on his assignments and discussions." To my amazement, and especially my sisters, the good man said, “Let’s give it a try”. I was so happy to be in my own grade. My sisters later proudly told my parents of my audacity in dealing with the principal. They thought I was very brave in arguing my case in broken English. I was now enrolled in a class of about 35-40 students, totally immersed in English. For the first few days, I was intimidated and overwhelmed. But, by the time the school year ended, I was fluent in English and passed grade four with very good grades. The principal had made the right decision. For me, this was a milestone for this reason: many immigrant children were placed in lower grades and many, if not most, never went on to graduate from high school because they felt uncomfortable and never fit in. Consequently, they chose to quit school at the minimum age of 15 or 16. They would enter the job market in the most menial and unskilled jobs available to them. Except for the principal’s decision to accept my bold initiative whereby I was advanced to fourth grade, I may well have joined the ranks of these unfortunates.

Anyway, by the time I finished fourth grade, I had established myself in school, to such an extent that I looked forward to school and hated weekends because I'd be out on the farm with nothing to do the whole weekend except go to a Mennonite church service on Sunday, which I loathed, mainly because we were not Mennonites. Here in Coaldale, there were even more what I would call fanatical Mennonites including our relatives. I recall Sunday morning dressing and waiting for cousin George to arrive, then crowding into his car and going to the church. There, the adults would join the main assembly while kids would go to Sunday school. I hated Sunday school where I would see the kids that were jerks in school show up dressed to the hilt and acting like true angels. Those little hypocrites. After Sunday school, the kids were admitted to the main assembly to hear some long-winded minister preach negatively about the Catholic Church and in atrocious German to boot. The only worthwhile thing about these services was that they did eventually end and were followed by some good food offerings in the basement. My whole family hated going to that church under false pretense, except Grandma who was a

Mennonite to her death. Eventually, Mother had enough of this charade, and at a gathering of relatives and neighbors, she announced in public, what was known in private, namely that we were Roman Catholic and henceforth would no longer attend their service. A huge collective burden was lifted from the family's shoulders and we all felt so very relieved.

On the other hand, relatives and neighbors were very upset, with some shunning us while others criticized or made fun of us calling us various and sundry names. We couldn't care less and ignored the indignities. We now walked three and a half miles to the Catholic church in Coaldale, and did so happily, singing and chatting all the way there and back. Not only did we walk to church on Sundays, but we did our shopping in Coaldale and had to carry all our purchases back. Often Mom also would give Helen and Lydia a list of goods she needed. They then would go shopping during the school lunch hour and bring it home on the bus after school. As was the case in New Gem, we were able to grow most of our vegetables and meats. Dairy products came from our livestock. It was mainly dry goods and such staples as flour and sugar that had to come from a store. Late in 1949, Dad bought our very first car, a 1937 Chevrolet. That not only made trips to Coaldale easier, but made it possible to drive to the great metropolis of Lethbridge (population 20 to 25,000) for much expanded shopping possibilities. That 1037 Chevy had to be cranked to start it, and come cold weather it became all but impossible to start. I recall Dad taking out the battery and keeping it in the house. He would cover the engine with cardboard and old blankets. Even then, starting it was difficult.

But I'm getting way ahead of myself. Getting back to our arrival in Coaldale, it wasn't long after settling down that time came to thin and hoe the beet fields. Cousin George had landed about 10 to 15 acres of beets and prepared a contract with Dad that for about $500, we would thin and hoe them several times and finally harvest them in fall. Then and only then would we receive our $500.

Now from what we learned in later years, cousin George was not the best farmer in Coaldale, nor was his land the best.

And so, when he planted the beets, and in order not to leave any spaces he put down seeds way in excess of what was needed. As a result, when the plants emerged from the earth, they were as thick as a brush mat! Add to this a glut of weeds due to insufficient herbicide and we probably ended up working not only the worst beet fields in all of Coaldale, but all of southern Alberta. When you hoed and thinned the beets, you had to spaces them at the rate of one sprout every 12 inches. Everything else including weeds and thousands of other beet spreaders had to be hoed out or pulled out by hand. This was very slow, very tedious, and backbreaking because you were always stooped over while thinning. And because of the over-planting, you ended up hand picking the excess plants and weeds, because you could only thin so much with the hoe. Fortunately for me, I was too young to actually do the job and so spent only weekdays and after school hours doing beets. Mom, Dad and the girls worked all day, every day, with the girls having to skip school during the beet season. By the end of the day, you couldn't straighten up. Then poor mom would have to prepare supper, dad with my help, would take care of the animals, while poor Helen and Lydia would do homework they had missed. Speaking of my sisters, not only did they work in the beet fields, but before going to the fields they had to milk cows for cousin George which took about two hours and was done by hand. They did this all year and all the while we lived on that farm. They had it rough. Through my sister Helen, sister Rose found a job at Dr. McLean's in Pincher Creek doing housework and babysitting.

I don't recall how long it took to do the beets, but I assure you it took us twice as long as it would have, had fate been kinder and placed us on a farm with better land and a better farmer. But such was not our fate. After the first hoeing we got a few weeks break before going out for a second hoeing. On a good farm, the second hoeing is very easy and of short duration, but because of the profusion of weeds the second hoeing took us two or three times as long as it should have on a normal field. Not only did it take longer, but a third hoeing was required. By this time the beet plants in our fields weren't nearly as healthy as they should be. The reason was not enough fertilizer and the nutrients were going to weeds instead of to the beet plants. This was very obvious to both my parents, who after all had grown up on farms and understood the need for fertilizer to feed the crops and herbicides and insecticides to kill the parasites and weeds. Dad always said you can equate the yield of a crop to the amount of money you spent on fertilizer, herbicides, and insecticides and the amount of work invested. To say cousin George was a poor farmer is an understatement. Unfortunately, we suffered in terms of toil and sweat because of it and never, never were compensated for all the extra work. On weekends, Helen often had to help with cleaning house, mending socks, or babysitting at George Kopp's place.

After the beets were harvested about the end of October, Helen hitchhiked to Lethbridge to look for a job for dad. She walked from business to business and finally at a railway station office found a job for him. An appointment was made for dad to come for an interview. Dad got a job on the Canadian Pacific Railway on an "extra gang". This kept him from home for weeks at a time as they worked all over, and lived in special railcars that were moved to whatever worksite they shifted to. This work lasted only until it became too cold to work the rails. Dad would then go on unemployment until work again became available the following spring. In the winter and while unemployed, dad would go to evening school to learn English. He instinctively knew the importance of learning the language and embraced it with gusto and enthusiasm. He spent many hours quizzing my sisters and me with questions of spelling and pronunciation. The process of teaching a parent is a humbling experience in that the process is reversed i.e. a parent teaches a child, not vice versa. It both chastened and saddened me because somehow it placed me in an unwanted and unsolicited superior role to dad. That was not good.

Now while Dad was taking lessons and dealing with people, mother was strapped at home. Her contact with people was mostly with relatives and/or neighbors who spoke German. Thus there was little opportunity to learn English except what she could glean from us kids, who by now spoke English amongst ourselves and German with our parents. She picked up bits and pieces from our dialogue or by having us translate script and/or telling her how to pronounce words and to shape phrases. And so it was that one day mother asked me how to say, "it's not necessary". This was for the eventuality that she might have to tell someone that something was not necessary. I don't know what made me do it, but my reply was "you say 'it's nots ntez, tzary;" and I made her repeat it until she said it just as I told her, all the while giggling unmercifully inside. I thought that after I had had my jollies I would fess up and tell her the correct pronunciation. Well, somehow the subject at hand changed and I forgot about my devilish prank. Sometime much later in some forgotten setting I heard my mother proudly blurt out to an unbelieving person "It's not netz, tzary". The person that mom addressed had the strangest look on her face, and I with mouth open shrunk into the background pretending I didn't know mom. Later on when I told mom of the terrible thing I had done to her, she wouldn't believe me and I had a heck of a time convincing her. Only after telling the whole family, and after suffering through a moment of embarrassment and with the help of my sisters she was convinced of the proper pronunciation. To this day, this little saga elicits a goodly amount of laughter. It took a long time before mother trusted my tutoring again.

Getting back to summer of 1949; summer for me was boring. Not much to do. Occasionally I would go to the neighbors who lived within a mile radius. But most of them had kids either too young for me or too old, in which case they already had to help work on the farm.

Fortunately, summer vacation was only two months long. So although it seemed forever, it really wasn't that long. When you subtract about three weeks for catechism classes during that time, it shortened the summer even more. I rode an old, old bike that dad had gotten me very cheaply from a neighbor. Seems I walked or pushed that bike more than I rode it. I recall once after catechism that I had a flat tire. So I took it to a service station to put in some air. Well, I had seen men put in air in the tire by pushing the air nozzle on the tire air-valve and holding it there for a while. So I followed suit, but shortly there was a loud bang and a hole had ripped not only the tube, but the tire as well. To me this spelled disaster, because I knew the tube and tire were beyond patching and I doubted dad would bother buying a tube and tire for this wreck of a bike. And I was right. Dad wasn't angry and did not admonish me, stating only the obvious. And so my traveling was again limited to walking.

In fall (About September 1) to my delight, school started again. It was good to see friends and teachers again, even to learn again. But too soon came time to harvest the beet crop. This would have been the end of September, beginning October. By now, it was cold and the ground had frozen. In an effort to increase the yield, cousin George had irrigated the beets prior to harvest. Well, then the frost hit and then came time to dig up the beets, clean them, and chop off the leaves. This is done by digging up row after row of beets by a tractor-pulled machine. Then we, the beet workers, followed to pick up the beets by the leaves, bang them together to knock off the clinging dirt, and then throw them on piles. This is hard enough under favorable conditions, but as usual, conditions on this farm were never favorable. As stated earlier, George had irrigated prior to the frost and harvest. Because of that, when you picked up the beets, a large chunk of mud or dirt clung to the beets. It seemed like you had a 25 or 50 lb. weight in each hand and you had to bang these two weights together, again and again until all the dirt was knocked off the beets. This was very hard work and before long, hands, wrists, and back were so sore you could hardly move them. After knocking the dirt off the beets and piling them up into mounds at intervals of 15 to 20 feet, you would pick up a machete which was about 18" long and two and a half inches wide and had a sharp quarter inch diameter thick and four inch curved hook on the end. The handle end had a strap with a loop that fit over the wrist and served to share the weight of the beet and prevent the machete from slipping out of our hands, weakened from fatigue. You would swing the machete in such a fashion as to drive the hook into the beet. You would then raise the beet and its leaves to your other hand, which would hold the beet firmly while you extracted the hook, then raise the machete and chop off the leaves. The beets would then be tossed into a pile, while the leaves would remain where they fell. A truck would later come back to pick up the beets. They were picked off the ground with special forks. Dad would help George in picking up the beets. By the way, the leaves were picked up later and stashed and fed to the cows in the following months.

This work was hard under the best circumstances, which did not exist on this farm. We would get up early in the morning, when it was cold, with snow on the ground at times. We had special gloves that had a rubber coating to keep your hands dry, but because of that they were very stiff and clumsy, making it hard to grab the beets, especially for women and kids whose hands were smaller. And so, not infrequently while chopping off the leaves, you would cut into the globe and moisture and the cold would penetrate the glove and make for miserable hands.

This as dangerous work. I recall once during the season that Lydia, who was very fast and a very good worker, chopped right into her left index finger. It was a nasty cut that went to the bone. After bandaging it, she incredibly kept on working. We all felt very bad for Lydia and to this day the scar from that ugly accident remains. I too had an accident once while "chopping" beets as we called it. While thrusting the machete to spear a beet, it bounced off the beet and the point of the hooks slammed into my left shin. There was little bleeding and just a little point where the hook broke the skin, but that shin was sore and for a long time every step I took was accompanied by a painful twinge in my shin.

When I speak of the hard and miserable beet work let it be clear that my experience was nothing compared to that of the adults (including Helen and Lydia). For one thing, I helped only after school and on Saturday (we never worked on Sundays in those days). Thus I suffered the dismally cold morning only on Saturdays. Even on school days I was sent in from the field to do some minor chores in preparation for making dinner when Mom came in. I would also get the animals into the barn and feed them. The others were out there every day, until the beet crop was completely harvested. As can be imagined, everybody looked toward the last day with great anticipation and when it finally arrived there was much rejoicing.

One final comment on the beet work. You will recall that good old cousin George had contracted our service for $500 to be paid at the conclusion of the harvest. Well, lo and behold, the harvest was below expectations (surprise, surprise) and so he reduced our settlement to $350. A bit cruel, don't you think? The low yield crop was the result of his poor farming and it was his mistake that made our work so difficult. We should have been compensated more, not less. But in our state of poverty we didn't have any leverage in protesting the cutback let alone demanding more. And so we had no choice but to bite the bullet and accept the cut in cooperation. By today's standards a $150 cut may seem insignificant, but that sum could sustain our family for about four months in that time.

We remained with "cousin" George for two beet crops, from spring of 1949 to spring of 1951. The second season was a little easier for two reasons. One was the previous year's experience, which if nothing else lowered our expectations and that toughened us for the difficult task ahead. The other and more practical was that cousin George didn't repeat his previous mistakes, thereby making the work faster and less difficult. However, relations between our family and cousin George deteriorated. First there was the initially injury caused by his unilaterally cutting our compensation package. Add to that the fact that not only did Helen and Lydia milk the cows twice a day, but gradually to their dismay they also had to feed the cows, clean all the milking equipment and separate the cream from the milk (a slow process). Also, a promise to insulate our "shack", put siding on it and to repair the leaking roof never materialized. Neither did a promise to dig a cistern so we could store fresh water and we continued using infested irrigation ditch water until the day we left. Then a major sticking point remained- our Catholic religion. Our Mennonite brethren shunned us to put it mildly (outraged is probably more accurate). Thus it came time to look for something better, but what? Jobs were extremely scarce. The only sure thing was work in the fields, supplemented by part time work for Dad in the warmer months. These jobs could be anything from digging ditches, extra gang on railroads, some construction work, working as a farmhand on farms during the busy planting, and/or harvest season. It was while working for other farmers that Dad found that a lot of the farms, especially those owned by Czech or Hungarian farmers, were far more productive and far easier to work than Cousin George Kopp's farm. While working part-time on the farm of a Mr. Harris, dad was offered a beet work contract that included use of a house, as well as feed and shelter for our animals. Before accepting the offer, Dad consulted with the family. In view of deteriorating relations with cousin George and to avoid overt hostility, my family decided unanimously to make the move. And so in the spring of 1951 we moved our household and livestock to the Even Harris farm.

The Evan Harris's had two boys younger than me. We did not live on his homestead, but rather on his parents' homestead about a half mile from Evan's place. His parents had a stepson LaVerne (half brother to Evan) who was my age. So with LaVerne and Evan's two boys, I was no longer bored stiff. There was always something to mess around with after school, including a few chores. Although the shack we live in now was a two-room shack, infested with mice, we felt more comfortable than we ever did at cousin George's farm. The Harris's treated us well and there was a mutual feeling of respect. Add to this, we were much closer to town, making the walking distance to church, shops, and in the case of Dad's jobs, much shorter.

Hoeing the beets was a breeze, with much softer ground and a lot fewer weeds to contend with. Hoeing was easier and faster with less back bending resulting in less backache and stiffness. While the family worked in the fields, Dad had a job planting crops for a "Mr. Huber" who was a contract planter whereby for a fee he provided the equipment and personnel to plant beets, which required special equipment. Dad was paid by the acres planted and so he began early and worked late in order to maximize his pay. Since the planting lasted only about a month, he had to make the most of it. When the planting was done, he joined us in the fields while looking for another job.

By this time (spring 1951) we had managed to scrape up enough money to pay the MCC for our Atlantic crossing. For Mom and Dad, a big weight was removed from their backs. Now the focus of the family became a home of our very own. Afer all the "shacks" we had and were living in, my mother's only wish in life was to "have our very own house". And so sometime in the summer of 1951, to everyone's great delight, Dad purchased a lot in Coaldale for "our very own home". In about three years we were able to scrape together enough to pay off our loathsome debt, buy a lot for a house and had enough left over to begin building a house. This despite only part time work for Dad. So how did we do it? By saving and scrimping. There were no frills. Everybody pitched in, not only in doing the beets, but in summer both Helen and Lydia worked as nannies until school started. Rose was a full-time cleaning woman. My Aunt Helen made contributions to help support Grandma. Even I worked in bean fields in the summer, picking beans at two cents per pound. All our earnings were put into the family kitty. Spending was kept to a minimum. Christmas and birthday gifts were always practical things such as clothes or items needed in school. I had very few toys and most of the toys I had were probably handmade. I recall seeing this Sears catalogue and marveling at all the toys displayed there. At Christmas I would be allowed one gift within a certain price range and it would be hard to pick one of the myriad of toys displayed. I would look forward with great anticipation to receiving the gift at Christmas, but must admit to disappointment when finally receiving the toy comparing it what was displayed in the catalogue and what I had conjured up in my imagination.

Getting back to the summer of 1951, after buying the lot we had enough money to pour the concrete foundation for a house, which was done before the onset of frost. We did not have a full basement, but a small dugout was dug which would serve as a kind of cellar and storage space under the future house. During that summer I saw my first ever Western movie. Mrs. Harris took all of us kids to the movies. I was hooked on movies and there used to be matinees every Saturday. I remember admission was fifteen cents, a candy bar was five cents, and popcorn was also a nickel. So for a quarter I could pay for admission plus a candy bar and a bag of popcorn. What a deal! But how do you get a quarter? Money was scarce and there was no such thing as a weekly allowance in our family. Well, I learned that you could return empty pop bottles for two cents each and empty beer bottles for one cent each. I remembered while riding in the school bus or car I would see a lot of empty bottles in the ditches on either side of the roads. And I made the connection between the bottles in the ditches and the movies. A combination of pop and beer bottles totaling twenty-five cents would get me admitted to a matinee. And so, with a sack and a bike borrowed from one of the Harris kids, I would tour the main highways and byways collecting empty bottles until my gunnysack was full. I would turn in the empties at a grocery store and/or restaurant and be paid on the spot. This was quick and easy money and I always made a lot more than I needed.

Sorry for straying again from the summer of 1951. As already stated, we had managed to purchase a lot and to pour a foundation for our, oh so desperately, wished for "dream house". Further, and by far the best news that summer, dad applied for and from a large pool of applicants was offered the janitors job at Davidson elementary school in Coaldale. This was a dream come true. Since arriving in Canada, dad suffered through a series of temporary, menial jobs. In winter, there were no jobs at all, and the only source of income was from unemployed insurance and only if you qualified for it. Since most of Dad's part time jobs were in agriculture, an excluded classification, he was seldom eligible. Thus as janitor of the school, he had a full-time job that allowed him to stay at home and not worry about the next job, where it was or how long it would last. This was indeed a happy occasion for the whole family, which could now plan and act with a certainty that until then was not possible.

In the summer and fall of 1951, our house was taking shape under the expert supervision of a full-time carpenter, who together with the family had drawn up the blueprint of the house. It was a three-bedroom house, with living room and kitchen all on the first and main floor. A bathroom without plumbing served as my bedroom, as well as temporary bathroom (meaning it was used for washing and bathing only). My bed was nothing more than an army cot, and it had no closet or additional furniture, but it was mine and mine only. It was the first time in my life that I actually had my very own bedroom. One bedroom, actually the biggest was set up for grandmother.

A separate entrance form the porch gave her much needed privacy. Helen and Lydia slept in the second bedroom and Mom and Dad in the third. When Rose came home she was also with Helen and Lydia.

All of us spent time in the construction of the house. The carpenter did the big items such as the framing and roofing, and application of the plasterboard. All painting and inside finishing was done by us. Mother and Dad spent long, hard hours sanding and preparing the plasterboard for painting. Then they did the painting. We had no power, indoor plumbing or running water. We had an outhouse for sanitary functions. Imagine having to go to the bathroom at night or in winter when temperatures as low as minus 20 to 30 degrees were common. Your rear end would almost freeze to the slat. I remember using newspaper and/or magazines as toilet tissue.

We had no running water. To serve our water needs, we built a cistern. A cistern was nothing but a large hole in the ground lined with concrete and a 2' x 2' opening at the top. The cistern was filled by tanker trucks, which would be ordered several times a year when the water was about to be depleted. To get water from the cistern, you would take off the lid of the cistern and then lower a bucket on a rope, fill it, and then pull the full bucket back up. All our water needs were taken care of thus. Disposing of wastewater from bathing, laundry, and cooking involved simply dumping it in the garden. Solid waste was put in a man-made incinerator (nothing more than an oil barrel with the top cut off). Yes, life was simpler, but extremely cumbersome.

I am getting way ahead of myself again. Getting back to the spring and summer of 1951, it was for the family, and especially for me, a good year. Yes, we were jammed into a two-bedroom shack, but he Harris's were good and sociable people and we were left to do as we pleased. By this time, the only livestock we had was our faithful cow and a beautiful calf and both caused the family some grief. The cow, named "Meta", was like a member of the family. She was very gentle and obedient. While grazing far afield we needed only to call her name and she would come to the barn for milking, feeding, or whatever.

The grief with Meta came when we had to sell her, prior to moving into our own house. We all loved that cow and parting with her was a very difficult event for all of us. She was a good and willing friend that had supplied us with all our dairy needs, as well as producing a beautiful calf for us. That calf was about a year old Hereford, very sleek, with a beautiful color and face. We were preparing to sell it, making a good profit to help pay for our house, when disaster struck. We had allowed the calf to graze in the ditches alongside the road, where the grass always was longer and greener. Well, the calf was struck by a vehicle and severely injured. We never found out who struck it, but a neighbor found it lying motionless by the side of the road. We hauled it back to the barn and tried to make it comfortable on a thick layer of fresh straw. The calf breathed heavily and although there wasn't much damage apparent on the outside, the inside of the poor animal must have been all broken up and so after a 10-12 hour vigil by its side, stroking and comforting it, Dad finally convinced me that for its own sake, and to put it out of its misery, we should destroy it. So I left my friend, broken-hearted, never knowing nor caring how dad put it to sleep. That was another tough loss.

Fortunately, the pain of losing both our cow and calf was eased, if not erased, by the fun I had during this time playing and working on the farm with the Harris kids. It was here that I fired my first shotgun. It happened in the middle of the night, while three of us were spending a night together at the Harris house. After talking and horsing around half the night, one of the kids (not I) suggested we get up, take the shotgun and do some shooting. So, sure enough, we got up, raided the refrigerator, then grabbed the shotgun and shells and proceeded to go out to the field to shoot the gun. We went far enough to be out of earshot of the house, and then proceeded to set up a "shoot". Now, this gun was single-shot blunder, so after every shot you had to stop and reload. After every shot a shout of joy went up and I anxiously waited my turn. The other kids had shot the thing before and so, when my turn came, they told me that the thing had a big kick to it and to avoid a painful jolt, I should hold the gun firmly to my shoulder. I did as told and finally got to pull the trigger. There followed an explosion with a white flash, accompanied by a deafening boom. And the thing backfired so hard it almost knocked me over. I had a sore shoulder for several days, but the thrill of that blast has never left me. At this point, let me add that during my teenage years I went hunting quite often with my friends. I never killed any animal or bird by my choice, but I enjoyed the camaraderie of the hunt. I might mention that at all times did we handle our weapons with respect and we never left any animal or bird maimed or injured.

Living on a farm doesn't mean that you have fun all the time. No, indeed. Most of the time is spent working, but even that could be fun. For example, like all boys, I loved to drive the tractor and whenever offered a chance to do so, I would welcome the chance. After a field was plowed, I would do the raking which had the effect of disintegrating big clods of dirt. Then there would be the chance of pulling wagons or implements, but the job that brought the most fun was scattering manure. This involved filling an implement aptly called a manure-spreader with barnyard manure, then pulling it out to the field to be fertilized and spreading the manure all over. Two or three of us would load the spreader from a manure pile, take it out to the field, open the tractor full throttle, thus engaging the spreader at full speed. We would race across the field with manure flying all over the field as well as ourselves. We thought this was pure fun and always ran full out. When we returned for another load we got a stern warning from Mr. Harris to slow down, but that was only good until we got our next full spreader out to the field. We would go slowly for only a little while before the urge to "open-up" overcame us and away we'd fly. One day while flying away we hit a muddy patch that was not visible from a distance. By the time we saw it and applied the brakes, we were in the mud and in no time the tractor (was high-centered) bottomed out in the mud with wheels spinning wildly. Now we had a dilemma. We needed another tractor and a long chain to pull us out. The trouble was we had to engage Mr. Harris's services, knowing that by doing so we'd be admitting to speeding, which would lead to a much deserved barrage of verbal abuse and invective directed against us. Well, we had no choice and as we expected, when we apprised Mr. Harris of our dilemma he let loose a storm of invectives, the likes of which I have never heard again. We just stood there with the proper look of remorse and humility and waited out the storm. But whenever Mr. Harris turned his back, we'd sneak a glance at each other and grin like idiots knowing the bark was bigger than the bite. Once he caught us grinning and that loosed another and even hotter flood of invectives, most of which I had never heard before. In the end we did retrieve that stuck tractor and spreader for but for a week we didn't drive any tractor and were allowed only to shovel manure. That stunk, both literally and stark reality.

School too was going well for all of us. My grades were good and I enjoyed both the learning and the social aspects of school. By this time, I had discovered books and how intriguing they were. Books like "My Friendly Flutie" and "Black Beauty" were riveting. Once started, I couldn't put them down. One of the requirements in my literature (or English class) was to read ten books during the school year and to write a report on each. I recall having completed my ten books and reports in less than two months. I could never figure out why so many kids couldn't or wouldn't do their ten reports in a whole year. Some of those reports were taken from the jacket of the book or the summary. Anyway, I loved reading and found it to be an interesting pastime. This may have been due in great part to lack of television. My family did not have a television set until I finished high school. In fact, we got our first table radio when I was in grade seven or eight. Radio, too, could be a distraction from schoolwork in that I found myself listening to the hit parade and/or cowboy dramas like "Roy Rogers", Gene Autry's "The Lone Ranger", etc. etc. To their credit and mine, however, I would listen to these programs AFTER my homework was done. Doing homework first as well as my love for books was crucial, I believe, in my doing so well in school. Those traits were ingrained in me not only by my parents, but also by my sisters. How so?

The answer to that question had its genesis while living on George Kopp's farm and how bored I was with no friends to play with. Those that were my age were Mennonites with whom

I had a mutual distrust, bordering on dislike. Well, it was during one boring moment that Helen began telling Lydia and me the story or book she had been reading. While I became engrossed in her storytelling, Helen became (to me anyway) a spellbinding storyteller. After a while, Lydia too began describing her latest book. And so it was that I decided I wanted to read my own books. The only ones available were from a collection of books that were kept on a bookshelf in my classroom. I asked my teacher if I could take home a book and she encouraged 'by all means' to take home a book whenever I wanted, requesting only that I would bring it back when finished. And so began my interest in books.

While on the subject of school, this was also a time to hone or nurture my love for music. Again, my family was instrumental. Although all the time we lived on a farm we had neither radio nor television, we all loved music and would sing together or individually whenever the spirit would move us. I remember drifting off to sleep many a night with Helen and Lydia singing duets while lying in bed. (Remember both at

Kopp's and at the Harris's, Helen and Lydia slept together in one bed and I slept in another). They sounded very good and I often joined them, encouraged by my parents from another room. We sang German songs and English songs, sad songs, and happy songs, funny songs, and silly songs. Mixed in with the songs were poems and gossip. We were really blessed with ample dialogue and communication in sharing our life's experiences as well as sharing unity and harmony with family. That doesn't mean there weren't disagreements and spats. There were! I didn't like teasing which Lydia was wont to do. On the other hand, I loved to tease Lydia and recall an incident where she lashed out at me by throwing a table fork at me, missing my head by inches and ending up stuck in the wall. Boy, did she get a tongue lashing from Mother. Mother's basic message to Lydia and all of us was: "don't ever throw dangerous missiles at anyone; use your hand or quick kick in the ass or better yet, let mother handle it". So much for that. As far as Helen was concerned, I recall spats or tiffs, but I was just a little wary of her because her way of inflicting punishment was to pinch, and pinch hard. I remember more than once screaming out after a particularly painful pinch and thinking of wreaking revenge someday “when I grew up”. That last phrase had its origin in some advice my mother once gave me. It happened after a painful incident after which I complained to mom and asked her to mete out appropriate punishment. Mother, probably knowing that I deserved the punishment, would tell me “wait until you grow up, then you’ll be strong and able to beat up your sister!” I was satisfied with this advice, and would repeat it loud and clear every time my sister beat me up- “Wait until I grow up!” Yet sometimes I would ask myself, Mom’s grown up, so why doesn’t she beat them up? Well, I’ve been growing up for a long time and one of these days I’ll have to drive up to Canada and beat up Helen and Lydia to fulfill a promise I made to myself as a boy. Look out sisters- your day of reckoning is coming!

So much for spats with my sisters. In the fall of 1951, we harvested the beets. It was a good crop and everything went well and we were compensated appropriately. That should not imply that it was easy. It wasn’t. All beet work is backbreaking work, which since those days has been mercifully taken over by machines. And so we made our move to our very own house which by now was far from complete, but was inhabitable. The happiest member of the family was Mother. At last her dream had come true- we had our very own home- our own palace. We couldn't' believe the space. I for one no longer had to share a bedroom with my sisters or parents or Grandmother. And poor Grandmother, who was in her 70's, had a room all her own to rest in peace and quiet.

But much work remained, and was done bit-by-bit and project-by-project as funds allowed. First we painted all the rooms, and then we covered all the floors with linoleum. For a long time we had a coal stove in the kitchen and coal heater (no furnace) in the living room. This was a dirty business as coal had to be kept in a bucket at all times to feed the stove and heater. It also required ducts that took the smoke from stove and heater to the chimney and then to the outside. These ducts would have to be cleaned every so often as soot would build up inside of them. The whole length of the ductwork would have to be taken apart, section-by-section. Inevitably, some of the soot would fall out and leave hard-to-clean black spots on the floor and/or furniture. It was filthy and it was also dangerous in that the ducts would get awfully hot thereby presenting a fire hazard and/or fires could erupt inside the ducts if not kept clean. When gas was introduced in Coaldale, it was welcomed with gusto. I don't remember the year, and though it strained our financial resources, it received top priority for installation. This too was a momentous occasion for us – no more coal, no more soot and dust, no more ducts and no more buckets of coal in the cellar which had to be lugged upstairs, several times every day.

The next big event was installation of water and sewer lines. This too was cost intensive, and yet it was an essential element in improving our lives. So there was no hesitation in signing up for hook-up to the town water and sewage facility. The financial strain can best be understood when you consider the cost of cutting an eight foot trench (depth required because of frost conditions) from the street to the house, plus the cost of thc pipe, not only from street to house, but all the piping required inside the house, not to mention bathroom and kitchen sink facilities. I'm not sure, but I think Dad borrowed some money, or a financing arrangement was established by the town, enabling homeowners to pay their debt over time. Be that as it may, we now have indoor plumbing. No more freezing your ass in the outhouse. We could take a bath in a regular bathtub at any time of the day. No water to heat prior to pouring it into a wash bin. Just open the valve and 'presto', you had water, either hot or cold, after washing dishes, cooking or baking. There was no dirty water to be spilled while carrying it out and dumping it in the backyard. It was wonderful and it took a while for the novelty to wear off.

Sometime in the spring of 1952 we purchased a 1949 Pontiac hatchback. This was a significant moment, in that it now enabled us to travel beyond the town boundaries, which heretofore was possible only through public transportation, namely Greyhound bus and/or train, which ran on a once a day schedule. So now we could travel anywhere and at a time that suited our wishes. Thus, we could purchase both foodstuff and dry goods in Lethbridge where a much broader and cheaper inventory of goods was available. Another additional and huge benefit was the recreational activities the car made possible. We could travel to recreational sites to swim and fish, we could attend shows for entertainment and very importantly we could visit aunt Helen and Rose, both of whom still worked in Pincher Creek. It opened up a whole new world for us, and for me especially, it was a Godsend. The thrill of learning to drive that car and bragging about it as boys want to do, was a dream come true. It had an automatic gearshift which at the time was very novel and worth bragging about.

Now just a few words about the town of Coaldale in those years. Coaldale had a population of less than 2,000. A provincial highway ran through town and the commercial district on Main Street was limited to a four-block distance right along the highway. It was the only street that was paved. The rest of the town (residential) had neither asphalt nor even gravel. This also was true of all country roads. You can't imagine the problems it caused when it rained. Cars were always getting stuck up to their axles. Most of the time two or three people could push them out but not without getting dirty from the top to bottom or being sprayed with mud as the car finally took off. Thus on rainy or muddy days you would always wear galoshes or over-boots that fitted over the shoes and would be scraped on a special grate outside most establishments before being removed and stored in a special place at the entrance. You may recall me earlier mentioning a porch in our new house. Well, all houses used to have a porch (or ante-room) and its main purpose was so that once you've entered it, you could leave your dirty boots and clothes in this porch before entering the house. They were absolute musts and also served as a storage area for water buckets, baskets, and other tools and supplies, which were necessary evils in the time and before the introduction of power, water, sewage, and gas. Eventually after installation of those amenities, the need for porches disappeared and houses built after 1952 did not include porches.

While getting stuck in the mud during the rainy season was bad enough, the situation wasn't much better during the snow season, with cars slipping and sliding in along the streets and getting stuck in deep snow. While getting stuck in the mud during the rainy season was bad enough, the situation wasn't much better during the snow season, with cars slipping and sliding along the streets and getting stuck in deep snow. Again, several persons could push them onto more firm ground, and though the whole effort was cleaner than was the case with mud; again you would be sprayed with cold and wet snow when the vehicle eventually spun away. Oh, such wonderful adventures! Don't miss them for a second.

Eventually, as mentioned earlier, Coaldale did receive public utilities and also graveled its streets. That was a huge step forward. Oh, gravel created its own problems, i.e. flying gravel broke many windshields, but on balance, its advantages far outweighed its downfalls. Vehicles simply aren't designed to function in mud and everyone was happy at the demise or end of mud roads. Many years later after I had left town, Coaldale paved its streets with asphalt and also built a network of sidewalks. It has turned out to be a neat, modern town in the intervening years.

By now, 1952, I was in grade seven, Lydia in grade nine, and Helen in eleventh grade. We had by now assimilated into mainstream society. We felt at home, happy and content with our academics and social life as well as our spiritual life. Living in such a small town has some distinct advantages, chief among which is security. Until I was in high school, I didn't know we had a key to the house. In other words, we seldom locked our doors, doing so only when leaving town for several days. Everybody knew each other and their property. I can remember when walking the streets greeting everyone with a friendly "Hi" or "Hello" and calling out their name. There was a bit of a downside to this communal openness and that was that everyone knew what you did, so you better be on your best behavior. One personal incident will illustrate this point. Sometime during my high school years, I had a certain interest in a blonde girl and we had probably held hands in public or whatever. Well, one day my Dad came home from work and uncharacteristically ignored me, giving me only dirty looks during supper without so much as a world. I knew something was wrong, and I felt guilty but I couldn't for the world of me figure out what horrible thing I might have committed. And so I confronted him by asking him the cause of his sour mood. With a disgruntled snort he said, "We've always been telling you to be on your best behavior in public, because what you do is a reflection on the whole family. You've disgraced us." From his facial expression you could see that he was both hurt and very angry! However, being innocent and ignorant of any wrongdoing, I was indignant and asked him "What are you talking about?" To which he replied "I was talking with Mr. 'So and So' today, and he informed me that you have been carrying on with "that floozy" in public. I can't believe you lower yourself to that level." I laughed, but it took quite a bit of explaining, before I convinced Dad that I had never associated with that girl of questionable character, and that his informant had mistaken the girl he was me with, with "that floozy" who also happened to be blonde. A huge weight was lifted from Dad's shoulders, and he expressed his great relief and his pride in me. Sure glad we cleared that up. Thus knowing and being known by everybody can also have its drawbacks.

Our spiritual life too was flourishing. I had by now become an altar boy and enjoyed that privilege immensely. In time, I became head altar boy in charge of all the other altar boys. On major feasts such as Easter and Christmas, I was the Master of Ceremonies and enjoyed that task a lot. Another time I had to read the gospels, epistles, and announcements for the priest who had lost his voice for several months. My folks were very proud of the way I performed my duties- but more importantly it prepared me for talking and performing tasks in public without fear or nervousness. For Mom, the ever fervent, good Catholic, going to Mass every day was a blessing and she no longer regretted having left Germany. Dad liked his job not only because it provided work and income the year round, but he was in a school environment. Being a teacher, being in this environment was also a blessing. Both teachers and kids liked him and he was included in many of their activities, pleasing him to no end. The only downside to the job was that he'd have us; the sisters and me help him after school. I didn't like it, and never missed an opportunity to let Dad know it.

Because I didn't like working at Dad's school after school, I found various jobs that kept me busy after school. In the spring, I would sell garden seeds door to door and did quite well. In the fall and winter, I would sell Christmas cards, Easter cards, and magazines. Selling became quite easy for me, and more than a few of my customers told me "You are a heck of a salesman!" That was probably because I didn't give up easily on a sale. Anyway, in addition from saving me from working at Dad's school, I was able to make enough from these after school sales to buy my very first wristwatch and my first brand new bike. I was very proud of both and proudly showed them off. During the summer months I also continued picking beans, advancing to head foreman......

Addendum

By Helen (Siebert) van der Sloot

We are so grateful to Reinhard for taking the time and effort to write his biography. Unfortunately, he was not able to bring it to completion. In the request of his family, I will try to fill in the part from where he left off to the time he met his lovey wife, Lucy.

Reinhard continued to do well in school and it was always fun to have him around. He was full of life and energy and he got along well with everybody. His laugh was contagious and echoed through the house. When he laughed you had to laugh too even though you may not have known what he laughed about. Our family was a close-knit family. As we grew older we still continued to do a lot of things together. I remember our friends coming over and we would always play games together either outside in the summer or inside in the winter. We played cards, crokinole, and monopoly.

Reinhard, Lydia and I belonged to the church choir. Every week, we had to go to choir practice to prepare for the Sunday Mass. Besides singing hymns we also sang the Mass of the Angels which was sung in Gregorian chant. There were two or three more Masses we learned. They were all in Latin and we sang each in four parts. Our little choir (the Huber girls, some girls from Readymade, Gre Langenberg who had a very beautiful voice and some young men from our parish including Pete and Bert) under the direction of Kors Lieverse, sang very beautifully. We all enjoyed singing. Besides the choir we also were members of the CYO (Catholic Youth Organization). We had table tennis tournaments in our parish hall, we had corn roasts in the summer, and we often got together with other CYO's for spiritual events as well as for dances etc. We had a lot of fun.

Our family loved music (must have been inherited from both our parents). Dad played the guitar and we stood around him and sang. We also had a balalaika way back in the Ukraine. It was fun to play the instruments with some help from Dad.

During Junior High School Reinhard also studied the clarinet and played in the Coaldale Youth Band.

On September 3, Lydia and Pete were married and in the following year on August 18, Bert and I were married, Reinhard being in the wedding party for both weddings. He was still in high school at that time. Our dear sister Rose chose to stay single. Our families became her families too. It was a real blessing for my parents to have Rose at home especially when they got older, mother ridden with arthritis so badly that she could hardly walk. Rose brought a lot of sunshine into their home. She was always cheerful. Her nieces and nephews all loved her.

After completing High School, Reinhard attended the University of Alberta in Edmonton for a couple of years. At the end of this third year his marks were not up to par. Most likely it was due to an active social life! I am sure he was well aware of his shortcomings. How will he let his parents know? He knew that they had high expectations of him, and he certainly did not want to disappoint them. So it happened one night that he came straight from university to Burdett where we (Bert and I with our two children) lived. He needed compassion and moral support. We used to say during the war: "They can take everything away from us except our faith in God and our education." He was still young and it was quite obvious that he wanted to continue his studies. Reinhard stayed overnight and left for Coaldale the next morning. My parents were very understanding and we never ever heard anything more about it. I think Reinhard had learned a lesson and was all the more determined to go back to University and complete his degree. For one year he attended the University of British Columbia in Vancouver to study accounting; but by the end of the year he knew that that was not exactly what he liked. The following year he transferred to the University in Fort Wayne, Indiana (U.S.A.) on the recommendation of one of his friends. He enrolled in the chemical engineering department, the same as in Edmonton. There he graduated with flying colors. We certainly don't always know God's ways. It was meant for him to go to Fort Wayne. There at University he met Lucy Hoffman, his future wife. I remember him sending us a picture of her and we thought she looked like a movie star. Subsequently, during his summer holidays, he brought her home so that we could all meet her. Her brother, Carl, was sent along as a chaperone. That was the thing to do in those days. Thus the threesome drove north to Canada in Reinhard's stylish 1950's model convertible complete with fins. We were very happy to meet Lucy, our new sister-to-be and Carl. We were all impressed and knew Lucy would make a good wife and mother. We were also impressed with Carl and his sincerity. One of the memorable highlights of their trip was Reinhard's giving everyone rides in his fancy car, cruising down third avenue strip in Medicine Hat, driving a little beyond the speed limit to accentuate the breezes whipping back one's hair!

Reinhard was always a favorite of his nieces and nephews, probably because he was their "young uncle" who always had time for kids. Looking styling in his black pants, white socks, and crew cut, he would engage the young ones in mock football games, do magic tricks and tell jokes. Mom always used to say he loved to make fun.

While Reinhard and Lucy were living in Vancouver, Washington, they would sometimes come home to Coaldale for Christmas. Reinhard would always bring something he had newly discovered in his American setting to enliven the celebrations. One Christmas he brought a bottle of champagne. Anxious to enliven the excitement of the season, he popped the cork vigorously only to have the cork fly out of his hands, hit the light fixture and break it. A moment of silence ensued. Then as the bubbly began to flow freely, the incident was forgotten. However, the broken fixture in his parents' kitchen remained for a long time as a tribute to that memorable Christmas.

65958883R00178

Made in the USA
Lexington, KY
30 July 2017